Are you looking for a map to [?] detours, and through the scen[?] [?]arts of kindness? *Manners That Matter for Moms* is a current and friendly GPS designed specifically for you to navigate your children toward a genuine consideration for others, which is unquestionably the essence of manners. In this intimate book written in mom-to-mom style, Maralee shares personal stories that span the gamut of our emotions and identify our unasked questions. As a mom of two boys, Maralee gets how hard it is today to raise gracious children in our often raw culture. This book will give you the how-to of making manners not merely a list of rules. Your children will never be stilted or performing. You'll find here how to make manners an easy, impressive way of life that benefits your child and your family and is in sync with how we live today.

Janie Upchurch
author of *Finding Herself Blessed*

One aspect of parenting is to craft with great intentionality children's behavior in order to shape their hearts. Manners build character. Start today with Maralee's book as your guide.

Ron Deal
author of *The Smart Stepfamily*
director, Blended Family Ministries and FamilyLife®

Manners that Matter for Moms covers the most important topics in child rearing in a light but informative way. The book was reassuring for me and is sure to be a blessing to young moms who want what is best for their children. At some point, we all come to the end of instructing our children and let them go into the world to make their own decisions. It's nice to see that our hard work of setting examples and instructing helps children become great adults. This book is a wonderful compass for moms.

Kim Alexis
supermodel, author, and TV host

Manners matter, and since our children will live in our homes only 21 percent of our lifetimes, it's essential that we reach them through simple daily connection points. In a time when manners seem all but forgotten, your children will have a huge advantage if you show them how to carry themselves wisely. Maralee McKee will teach you how to do that in this practical life-application resource, which systematically guides parents in building extremely successful kids.

Dwight Bain
director of the LifeWorks Group
executive director, International Christian Coaching Association

What a joy it is for me to endorse Maralee's new book on manners. I feel very strongly that America needs this information and encouragement so moms (and dads!) can teach their kids proper behavior. Maralee, in her warm, practical, and up-to-date style, shares simple skills children will need in order to flourish in our current culture. Young adults who haven't been exposed to these skills while growing up could also use this book. Regardless of your age, it will help you gain confidence in all your relationships. This information is broader than just etiquette. It takes so little to be above average, and this book will help you do that.

Emilie Barnes
founder of More Hours in My Day
author of more than 70 books

Maralee's writing is compassionate and completely engaging. This immensely helpful guide offers parents and children timeless principles for kindness, sensitivity, and courtesy in today's world.

Jan Parish
author of *Peak with Books* and *Doors to Discovery*
founder, Playful Early Learners

Want to give your child a social safety net? Maralee McKee shows how manners provide just that—they put us at ease and help us to put others at ease so that we can feel confident to go out and turn the world upside down for God!

Sheila Wray Gregoire
author, *To Love, Honor and Vacuum*

Manners That Matter for Moms

Maralee McKee

HARVEST HOUSE PUBLISHERS
EUGENE, OREGON

Cover by Dugan Design Group, Bloomington, Minnesota

Cover photos © Eric Audras / Getty Images; iStockphoto / JaniceRichard, Funwithfood; Fotolia

Backcover author photo Angela Robbins Hull, True Moxie LLC

Maralee McKee is represented by MacGregor Literary, Inc. of Hillsboro, Oregon

MANNERS THAT MATTER FOR MOMS
Copyright © 2012 by Maralee McKee
Published by Harvest House Publishers
Eugene, Oregon 97402
www.harvesthousepublishers.com

Library of Congress Cataloging-in-Publication Data
McKee, Maralee
    p.cm.
Includes bibliographical references (p.   ).
ISBN 978-0-7369-4489-2 (pbk.)
ISBN 978-0-7369-4490-8 (eBook)
1. Etiquette for children and teenagers. I Title.
BJ1857.C5M385 2012
395.1'22—dc23

                                                    2012009821

With gratitude and love I dedicate this book…

To Lisa Williams,
who first opened the door and invited me in.
Every door that has opened for me since has been a direct result
of your enthusiasm for helping people live out graciousness and
Christlikeness and your belief that I was the person to deliver the
Manners Mentor message.

To Marsha Dickinson
This book exists because you kept telling me this day would come!
Through the gifts of your friendship, encouragement, and prayers,
you gave me the courage I needed to write.

And to Kent, Marc, and Corbett
I'm honored to be called Kent's wife and Marc and Corbett's
mom. You are my greatest joys, and our family is my greatest
blessing. McKees…together forever!

Contents

Foreword

What an honor it is for me to introduce my dear friend Maralee to you! I only wish I could do so in person, but believe me, you holding this book is the next best thing.

If you don't know her yet, you might be reading this first page with a bit of trepidation. I can hear the thoughts now: "A book about manners for kids? But I'll bet Maralee's children are perfect. She has no idea what my kids are like! She couldn't possibly understand the challenges I face!"

Relax and take a breath. I've known Maralee and her family for years. Our families have vacationed together, ridden roller coasters together, eaten french fries with extra ketchup together, and hosted slumber parties for each other's kids. I can tell you that her boys are well-mannered and kind, but that doesn't mean they're perfect or that Maralee expects them or anyone else to be. The McKees are actually one of the most relaxed and fun families we know. In fact, when you read this book you're in for a unexpected treat—learning the real meaning of manners, which has nothing to do with attaining perfection or expecting it from others.

However, the first time we ever vacationed with the McKees, I'll admit I was a little nervous too. I had known Maralee and her wonderful family for a while, but there was still that "Oh my goodness—she's the Manners Mentor" fear. That was before I knew Maralee's genuine brand of manners and only knew the rigid, judgmental stereotypes we see on sitcoms or read about in outdated books.

I was understandably concerned about my children's behavior in front of her. I lectured them on being calm for our new friend and did my best to rein in their excitement. The first restaurant we ate at together was a very nice one, which didn't ease my nerves one bit as I walked in the dining room with my five-year-old. Katy Rose was on a roll right out of the gate. Excited to be in a fancy restaurant, she chattered on about the linens and decor in her typical outdoor voice.

I was trying to remind her to turn the volume down just as our servers arrived with our entrees. Suddenly she popped out of her seat and bounded over to Maralee in excitement. She dramatically opened her mouth, gestured toward her lower jaw, and exclaimed, "Miss Maralee! Miss Maralee! My tooth is loose! Wanna wiggle it?"

My husband and I were ready to crawl under the table in embarrassment. Without missing a beat, Maralee put down her fork, turned to Katy Rose with a big smile, and said, "How exciting! I'd love to wiggle your tooth, Katy Rose!" My child had never been prouder in her entire life.

Maralee won her over instantly, and Katy Rose has loved her ever since. Even now, when Katy Rose and I go out to eat, she proudly shows me how Miss Maralee puts her napkin in her lap, and she loves to show me how to dispose of empty sugar packets like princesses do.

We all want the best for our kids, and we're all doing our best to raise them to be gracious and confident adults. I truly believe Maralee has the secret to doing just that, and I'm personally grateful that she has generously shared her wisdom with us.

In this book you'll discover how to teach your child to behave in public without nagging, how to set your children up for success by teaching them to interact well with others, and many more nuggets of wisdom (even including bathroom and bodily noise manners). You'll find yourself breathing easier with every chapter.

That's who Maralee is, and that's what manners are. They aren't a secret code that elite people use to quietly condemn others; they're a manner and way of treating people that set both them and you at ease.

Don't worry, Maralee isn't going to tell you what you're doing wrong or judge you if your children aren't perfect. Believe me, she's too real for that! Instead, you're going to discover a loving mother with a kindhearted understanding for everyone and a gift for explaining how to raise up considerate and confident children who display grace and kindness in any situation.

Christy Jordan
Author of SouthernPlate.com
Host of ABC's *Beat the Chef*

1

Moms like You and Me

Today our children are our shadow.
Tomorrow they will be our reflection.
MARALEE MCKEE

I was nervous. I wanted this evening to be perfect for my husband, who was hosting a client-appreciation dinner for his company. He had worked hard planning every detail—especially choosing the guest speaker. After some negotiating, the man he hoped would accept his invitation agreed to present the keynote address.

This gentleman is a financial genius. He holds three degrees—one each from Harvard, Yale, and Oxford. He consults privately with kings and presidents about global economic issues. All of this at the ripe old age of 34. He and I are about the same age, but I feared that was all we were going to have in common. A genius I'm not.

Common Ground

My husband planned to go from table to table, chatting with guests through dinner. That meant our special guest and I would share a cozy table for two throughout the 90-minute dinner before he took the stage. Driving to dinner, I was still trying to think of conversation topics he might enjoy and I would have an inkling about.

My list was short.

My concerns about us not having much common ground to talk were quickly realized—he was intense.

Moments after sitting down, he asked, "Maralee, I like to know my audience a little before I speak. What would you say are some of the economic and libertarian concessions you believe your guests are willing to make in light of our current financial and political surrounding?"

Okeydokey! Believe it or not, that particular question had not made my short list of conversation topics. Hiding my panic, I quickly decided that in order to survive this meal, I was going to have to be the one asking the questions.

I answered brightly, "I'm sure my husband will have more accurate insight than I do. I'll call him over in a minute." Then I asked our guest where he was from. He shared that he was born in Chicago and still lived there. I had recently visited for the first time and been smitten with the city. We began to find common ground talking about Chicago's famed Miracle Mile. A few minutes later I asked about his family. He beamed as he told me that he and his wife were expecting their first child the next month— a girl.

We talked about how children change everything. But then he added, "But only for a little while."

His genius was obvious in what he said next. It has been one of the most impacting maxims on the way I parent.

Twenty-One Percent of My Life

He explained, "We spend a statistically small percentage of our lives in direct contact with our children. Let's say I live to be eighty-five, and my daughter lives with my wife and me until she leaves for college at eighteen. In that case, we're only under the same roof for twenty-one percent of my life. Seventy-nine percent of it will be without daily contact."

My mind raced to make sense of it all. How can that be? Only 21 percent of my life will be spent sleeping under the same roof as each of my children?

The cold reality of the number made my heart shiver—it still does.

Twenty-one percent is all the time we have with our children, and that's if you start counting when they are newborns. If they're five or fifteen already, a measure of that time is gone.

Is it enough time to teach them everything they need to know to thrive on their own when they're grown? Yes it is, but they won't learn it by accident. If we want our children to grow into adults who interact with kindness, respect, self-control, graciousness, and friendliness, we must teach them a lost art in today's culture. It's the art of being intentionally kind and patient in the words they say and the things they do every day, everywhere, with everybody. Quite simply, we must teach manners.

Moms like You and Me

Because you're reading this page, I know you and I have some things in common. Moms like us deeply love our children and want to give them the skills they need to soar through life. We have high hopes for them—and not merely that they attend Ivy League schools, gain impressive-sounding job titles, win beauty pageants, or accumulate worldly wealth and fame.

Those are all fine things. But what matters more to you and me is that our children grow up to be kind, compassionate, friendly, warmhearted, caring, self-disciplined, self-controlled, self-reliant, fair, generous, empathetic, and even-tempered adults.

We wish them joy, so we want them to laugh daily and easily.

We want them to go with the flow but not to be easily swayed.

We want them to be optimistic but not to wear rose-colored glasses.

We want them to understand that personal conflict is inevitable but making enemies is optional.

We pray that they realize that apologizing for mistakes doesn't mean you're messed up. It means you have the strength of character to do the hard work of untangling messes.

We want our children to have a strong sense of right and wrong and the moral strength to live up to their convictions.

We want them to have goals and ambitions but not to let their goals become their gods.

We pray that they will always be secure in who they are so they don't become bullies or easy targets for bullies.

We want them to please people but not to be people pleasers.

And because mamas enjoy hearing good things about their children, if we notice ours displaying these traits, we won't mind a bit if people compliment them and tell us that our children are sweet and engaging and impressive. Christ within them makes all these things possible. Etiquette is the vehicle they'll use to express their character in word and deed.

Etiquette Is Kindness and Love in Action

The apostle Paul's famous passage about love in 1 Corinthians 13:4-5 lists nine attributes of love, and seven of them describe what love is not. That leaves only two positive descriptions of love: patience and kindness.

Etiquette is the language that expresses patience and kindness in our interactions with one another. It teaches us to make modest sacrifices of our time, our agenda, and our momentary wants so we can live out patience and kindness. Etiquette is not pretense or fussiness. It's not an attempt to make children perfect. Manners are the language of love, and we teach them to our children for their benefit and for God's glory.

Scripture often calls us to kindness. As Paul says in Ephesians 4:32 (NIV), "Be kind and compassionate to one another." Etiquette shows you how to live this way.

Etiquette Doesn't Replace Authenticity

I sincerely do not want to add stress to any mother's or child's life. When etiquette is forced or stressed, it's only on the outside. Love, on the other hand, is not forced.

We don't teach etiquette in order to mold children into something they are not. Some children are spontaneous, spirited, and quick to share their opinion. That's fantastic! They will grow up to be quick-witted, fun, welcoming leaders. Some children are reserved, slow to join in, and quiet. That's fantastic too! They will grow up to be thoughtful and always there for you—servant leaders of their generation. God gave our children their personalities. Etiquette gives them the skills to bring the best of their personalities to the forefront.

Etiquette Has Evolved

Gone are the days when manners were about debutante balls, seated dinners for 12 with the butler serving, hats and gloves, and making sure the children were seen but not heard.

The etiquette I share with you has evolved. It's in tune with the realities and sensibilities of our modern, casual, techno-savvy, fast-paced culture. Grandma's etiquette was perfect for her day. But if we use her etiquette exclusively, we're going to appear stiff and stuffy and out of sync for the time and place Christ has placed us in.

I've kept Grandma's timeless principles of courtesy, respect, hospitality, and consideration and used those principles to chart the course of our contemporary everyday encounters.

Etiquette Isn't Artificial

Some people say we shouldn't teach etiquette because by doing so we train people to be artificial. Not so. Rather than forcing us to wear false masks, etiquette frees us to become the best version of ourselves.

On the other hand, some people try to use etiquette to mold their children into perfect people. Perfection is Satan's trap. God didn't give us our children for our own glory but so that we could empower them to freely and gladly live for Christ and reflect His glory. Etiquette polishes us so that Christ's reflection can be seen more easily in us.

The skills you'll learn about in these pages aren't to be lived out legalistically. They are written in sand, not stone. You can use these principles to build and honor relationships inside and outside your family. This is an important concept. After all, the reason we were put here in the first place was to be in relationship with God and other people.

Etiquette Isn't Window Dressing

Motherhood gives us an opportunity to be the people we want our children to become. That's why I wrote this book—to help you teach your children and be a role model for them so their good manners spring from their hearts and are not just for show.

For manners to be more than window dressing in our lives, they must be expressed in the words we say and the things we do—and not just when we find it convenient or are in an especially good mood. Our good manners become true when they are ingrained into us, just as we can learn a new language and use it until it is as natural as our native tongue.

In the pages of this book you'll find the modern, essential skills you need to know and model to help your children soar through life free from social uneasiness so they can become well liked, well mannered, and well respected. None of it is hard to learn. All of it pays a lifetime of dividends.

Our Journey Together

I'm so glad we're going on this journey together! I've prayed and worked hard on this book for the benefit of you and your family. My prayer has been that it will encourage, inspire, and mentor you.

People often ask me how I became the Manners Mentor. It's a pretty amazing story. I can still barely believe I am where I am today.

When I was nine years old, I was in a situation no little girl should experience. At that time, I started praying for three specific things. Over the next 20 years, God answered my three prayers, slowly unfurling His plans and purposes for me in ways that even the most imaginative novelist could never conceive. I'll briefly share my story with you (friends should know about friends!) so you'll understand my passion for these skills and why I'm honored to bring you the message God has entrusted to me—that manners matter to Him.

In the teaching part of the book, I'll start by showing you how to teach etiquette without stressing or ever having to nag. We moms already have a lot on our plates. We don't need to pile more "must do's" on them. My way of teaching is gentle, subtle, and lifestyle-oriented. You won't find your children pushing back. Rather, you will see children who are more patient, kinder, and more likely to consider how their words and feelings impact the people around them.

You'll also find relevant, modern, indispensable tips on everything from table manners to texting. You'll learn how to make positive first impressions, interact with ease, and give and receive gifts graciously. You'll also learn about using Wonder Words, beginning and ending conversations on a high note, dining skills, table manners...all in sync with today's sensibilities and from the heart.

Chapters 4 through 17 start with just-for-fun etiquette IQ tests for moms. "Mom to Mom" tips start in chapter 5. These are special things that are on my heart to share with you. They're adult-level skills that will help you shine or special tips for teaching a particular skill set and touching the heart of your child.

Chapters 4 through 17 also include multiple sections titled "Growing in Graciousness (Next-Level Skills)." These next-level skills allow you to pick and choose what you want to add into the mix. You can introduce a particular skill whenever your children will benefit the most given their age and stage, natural bent (introvert or extrovert), personality, level of maturity, confidence, and degree of manual dexterity.

You might look at all these skills and say, "Wow, Maralee! That looks like a whole bunch. How can I teach all of that?" Let me assure you, you can! It's my joy to show you how. The skills you'll find here are the ones I've taught successfully in hundreds of my Manners Mentor classes. And of course, I use them at home with my own two sons, Marc and Corbett. These skills are classroom tested, and they work in the real world.

Just don't rush the process. You will teach and model for months or even years before some skills become parts of your child's life. That's normal. We're in it for the long haul, aren't we?

Our Shadow and Reflection

I often think of the evening years ago when I dined with the financial genius. Now that my two sons are nine and fifteen, his words resonate deeper than they did when he first showed me that children change everything "but only for a little while." We have 21 percent of our lives or less to daily impact theirs—just 21 percent to pass along to them everything they need to know to soar through life on their own.

The number one predictor of our children's future success and happiness is their ability to get along well with others, to be well liked, and to be confident and at ease in their interactions. You're holding in your hands the how-to's of instilling these character traits in your children.

Today our children are our shadow. Tomorrow they'll be our reflection. Let's embark on this journey together.

2

Twenty-Year Prayers

Our past doesn't define us. It prepares us.

MARALEE MCKEE

I've taught thousands of children in my Manners Mentor classes, and many of their moms have shared with me their own feelings of self-consciousness: "Maralee, I'm a nice person. I'm smart. I know that being able to interact well is important. That's why I sent my children to you. But I'm unsure about how to make a good impression myself. I often feel confused and stressed out."

I can identify with these moms because until about 12 years ago, I felt the same way. I didn't know what was expected of me in social situations, and every time I guessed, I seemed to get it wrong. Those experiences left me feeling awkward, lacking, and intimidated, so I kept to myself most of the time. My world was small—too small. I built my own jail cell to wall myself off from others. And when I gave myself a "get out of jail free" card and went out and about, even though I had a smile on my face, I was only masking my feelings of inferiority.

I'm Not Who You Imagine Me to Be

People tend to make assumptions about others. I know they make assumptions about me because they tell me they do. After they hear my story, people share their surprise—sometimes with tears. "I had no idea, Maralee. I assumed you knew about etiquette because you were from a

wealthy family or because your dad was a diplomat or something like that."
It's a reasonable assumption. It's just that my story is different.

For years when I was young, an evil man was in my life. He was a con
man. The stench of alcohol, cigarettes, and lust exuded from him and covered me—body and soul. I told no one. I smiled and was good and quiet,
and I stuffed the fear and shame inside and hid it well.

I knew God was real, but I didn't know whether He wanted to claim
me. After all, why would a glorious God want a tarnished anything? But
I kept begging Him, just in case. I prayed for three things throughout my
growing-up years: (1) that God would let me know if I was worthy of His
saving grace, (2) that He would bring good out of the bad I had experienced, and (3) that He would send me a prince. Who can blame a girl for
praying for her own Prince Charming?

My Prince Arrives

When I was 22 years old, I fell in love. We were engaged just ten days
after we met. I was shy, but he was talkative, expressive, intelligent, funny,
and deeply and passionately in love with God and with me. Before we sent
out our wedding invitations, I told him about my childhood and gave him
the opportunity to leave if he wanted. He cried for me and with me and
promised that we would grow old together.

Chuck was the son of a neurosurgeon. His family was in Orlando's
first *Blue Book Social Registry*. He was an only son, and his mother didn't
approve of me or my pedigree. She made it clear that he could have chosen a better wife and that she was hoping this marriage wouldn't last long.
However, not even she wanted it to end the way it did.

The week of our first wedding anniversary, Chuck was diagnosed with
terminal cancer and given a year to live. He survived almost five. They were
difficult years, full of hospital stays and chemotherapy and watching the
man I love, my prince, the man who showed me I was precious to God,
die a little bit each day. By the time I was 25, we had been fighting cancer for three years, and I became gripped with panic attacks so severe that
I thought I was going insane. I couldn't drive a car. It was difficult being in

public. I feared everything—especially what would happen if my husband died. And then my biggest fear came true. I was a widow at 27.

Prayers of a Stranger

My heart was shattered after my husband's death. I was alone with no dreams and no purpose. We had prayed without ceasing for his healing. We had prayed that we would have the children we named on our second date. When Chuck died, I clung to God but buried my dreams in the coffin with him. Every evening for months I cried my eyes dry by nine o'clock; then I would continue to sob without tears well into the night. Strangely, at about two in the morning a peace often came over me, and I would fall into a deep rest.

I didn't know that the week Chuck died, a bachelor named Kent McKee was on a prayer retreat, asking God to bring him clarity about getting married. He was 36 years old, and he couldn't understand why the Lord had not answered his prayer for a soul mate. God spoke to his heart and told him to go home—that He had answered his prayers and that he would soon meet his wife.

After that retreat, for weeks on end, Kent would awaken every night at about two a.m. When he woke, he would get on his knees beside his bed and pray because he sensed that his future wife was sad and afraid. He prayed that God would dry her tears and hold her close until he could comfort her.

"That's the Girl You Bring Home to Mom"

Eighteen months later, as I was still mourning my lost love, I was introduced to Kent at a friend's home. To my amazement, I immediately heard in my heart, "He's your forever husband." Twenty-one days later we were engaged.

Kent's father had also been a doctor, so I again felt as if I were an inferior intruder into a sophisticated world. The first time I met Kent's mom, I was a knotted tangle of nerves. Chuck's mother had never found favor in me. I wanted my marriage to Kent to be different, to be a union of families.

We met at her home for dinner. Between the entree and dessert I excused myself to use the restroom. Returning to the table, I passed by the kitchen, where Kent and his mom were dishing up slices of key lime pie. I just happened to be walking by at the moment his mother said to him, "Now, son, that's the girl you bring home to mom! She's the answer to my prayers." I held back tears of relief and joy and gratitude for Christ's good plans as I quietly slipped back to my seat.

My Purpose and Passion

Someday I'll write my life story. But this is an etiquette book, so I won't take up any more of your time except to tell you that God used my insecurities to lead me to an etiquette book. He took what I found most lacking in myself—my shyness, my feeling tarnished and unworthy to have a voice, my desire to disappear into the background—and changed it through prayer, Scripture, and an etiquette book. First one book, then five, then ten. After learning the skills in these books, I no longer felt as if I didn't deserve a place at the table.

Then He led me to share social skills through newspaper, radio, TV, and public speaking engagements. In time my fears of being in public were replaced with gratitude for having been given this message. My insecurities were replaced by a strong faith that He called me to do this and that He would equip me every step along the way. God had already answered two of my childhood prayers—He showed me that I was loved, and He brought me my Price Charming. This was the answer to my third childhood prayer—that God would bring good out of the bad I had experienced. Twenty years after I first prayed it, the Lord began to show me my unique purpose—to remind people that the way we treat each other matters to Him and to share the *how* (the etiquette) of being kind to one another.

I'm the most unlikely vessel for this message, but isn't that just like Christ? If we'll let Him, He'll take our pain and allow it to bear fruit in the most amazing ways. By His stripes I was healed of my insecurities, painful emotions, shame, and grief, and now through my stripes I can bring you this message.

The Christian's Special Call to Manners

Second Corinthians 5:20 (NIV) tells us, "We are therefore Christ's ambassadors, as though God were making his appeal through us."

My dictionary defines *ambassador* as "an official messenger with a special message." Wow! Doesn't that beautifully describe our job here on earth? We are to be Christ's ambassadors. The children of our nation's ambassadors are required to have special etiquette training for interacting with kindness and grace. How much more should you and I and our families take seriously our responsibility to represent Christ? When people see the way we interact with our family members, friends, and strangers, will they be drawn to what they see and want to join the family of Christ?

Jesus received positive feedback from others because of His behavior. Luke 2:52 (NIV) says, "And Jesus grew in wisdom and stature, and in favor with God and man." When our first priority is God, we will naturally find favor with men. As it was said of Jesus, may it be said of our children.

Our Special Call to Train with Christlike Love

As we train our children in etiquette, our own words and actions must be characterized by the same kindness and courtesy we are aiming to teach. Before I get into the etiquette training section of this book, I want to give you some key principles about training children that I've learned over the years. These are the same skills I'm using daily with my sons. These principles will show you how to teach etiquette without wearing yourself out, resorting to nagging, or having your children resent you. Etiquette taught in a Christlike spirit will be a blessing to your family, not a burden.

A Gentle Word and a Tender Way

Laws control the lesser man;
right conduct controls the greater one.
MARK TWAIN

Our house was built in 1952. In the backyard is a giant oak tree the original owners planted the same year. I adore that big old tree.

In summer, its wide, shady limbs shelter my sons when they play on the swing set and trampoline. In spring, its leaves rustle in the wind and calm my spirit. In the fall, those leaves rain down in a pageant of crimson and gold. It delights my eyes. Each winter, although the season doesn't get terribly cold in Florida, I'm comforted to know that squirrels and birds are as snug and warm in its boughs as my family is in our home.

I enjoy the life and beauty in our lovely oak today because someone else did the work of planting and carefully cultivating it a long time ago. So it is with our children.

What seeds am I planting or seedlings am I nurturing that will benefit those who come behind me half a century from now? I have my ministry, writing, and business. Those are all good things. They'll outlive me, Lord willing. However, they don't come close to matching my two most special blessings—my children. God could have chosen anyone to be their mother, but He honored me with that position. Likewise, He's honored you with your family.

With the honor of motherhood comes a sacred contract to tend to these children on loan to us. They've been placed in our care so their bodies and character can be nourished and prepared for God's plans, purposes, and approval. For me, it's a hard task. I don't have a green thumb. Yet I've been called to care for two of His most beloved creations—children made in His likeness, saved by the Father through the sacrifice of His own Son. I wonder (and worry)—am I planting the seeds in their hearts that will help them become caring, confident, and thoughtful adults who will be as deep-rooted as our oak tree and able to stand strong in Him for 50 years and more?

Heart to Heart

Do I fertilize my children's character enough by my praise and encouragement? Through listening, noticing, and being in the moment with them, do I protect them from the pests and insects of this world that try to eat away the tender sprouts of their thoughtfulness and gentleness? Do I do the hard and delicate work of pruning back their rude impulses, selfish wants, and vanity so they can grow a bountiful heart crop of service, unselfishness, self-control, gentleness, patience, and kindness?

Do you ask these questions too? Do you find that cultivating your children's hearts is labor intensive?

There's no magic wand to give me the extra pep I need on hard days when I'm frazzled. Sometimes I would rather turn on the TV and escape than read another storybook aloud to my youngest boy or pay attention to one of his lengthy tales about recent high jinks on the school playground.

And when I'm tired, it would be easier to give in just this once when my young teenage son begs, "But, Mom! I really want this video game. I know it's rated Mature, but it's not going to hurt me. I've heard bad words before on TV. I don't say them now and I won't from playing this game. Why can't I have it?"

Depending on the moment, I want to cry or snap or both.

But most times I pause, take a deep breath, and say a silent prayer. Then I listen, prune, fertilize, or do whatever work of love is needed at the moment. And I do it because I want more than a "because I said so" relationship with my children. I know that to touch their hearts for eternity, my words need to be gentle and my ways tender.

Sure, first-time obedience is expected in our home. But I am mindful that obedience applies only to their actions; I want them to *want* to do good, thoughtful things. And I know that children are most likely to develop the "want to" from authority that is kind and patient and selfless. So that's the kind of mom I try to be. Some hours I succeed. Some I fail miserably.

In the good moments, I show my children that I'm here for them by leaning in, listening, making eye contact, and putting aside whatever I'm doing to be totally in the moment with them. When I mess up in life, Christ gently guides me back with a tender spirit. I want to do the same with my children.

Keeping Rebellion at Bay

Did you know that manners are much easier caught than taught? If we'll engage in prayer-filled, consistent, loving, gentle, heart-to-heart communication with our children, and if we give them enough time and encouragement, our manners will be grafted into their hearts.

Sure, your child's will or temperament will sometimes conflict with the rules and manners of your home. Children naturally test their boundaries. However, more often than not, they will grow up to mirror your heart and attitude toward others.

Moms have often called or e-mailed me for advice about children or teens who refuse to learn manners. When this happens, the problem doesn't usually have to do with the behavior itself. Rather, the parent and child often don't have a relationship of mutual respect. They are not connecting heart to heart. Without this connection, good manners won't take root. The child will see the manners only as a long list of rules, and rules without relationship in a home lead to rebellion and resentment.

So once we have a firm foundation of relationship, how do we go about teaching manners to our children?

Let's look at eight core principles that will keep our hearts in the right place so we can lead our children well. Then we can instill actions and attitudes that will make the language of kindness their native tongue. We'll start with the principle that is absolutely indispensable for teaching manners—modeling.

1. Model What You Want to See Duplicated

Our character is formed at home, and because we want our children's manners to express their character and not conceal it, home is where we must first teach, model, and require manners.

Manners aren't learned over a few weeks; they are caught from the cradle to college. Your children will pick up your manners more reliably than they pick up your accent. Through your modeling, they will learn that they should look and smile at the people they converse with, that raising their voice is something to be done rarely, and that people aren't an interruption in your day.

When they see that you enjoy being courteous, they are much more likely to copy you without you reminding (nagging!) them. This is reinforced when they see how others respond with kindness and gratitude in return.

If the relationships between husband and wife, parents and children, and brothers and sisters aren't mannerly, rarely will children transcend their home life to walk confidently into the world and express goodwill toward others. It's hard to get water from a well that's almost dry.

Did you ever think about praying about manners with your children? Ask God to bless your family as you seek to live out graciousness and reflect Christ in your encounters. With your children, pray about the way your family interacts with, responds to, and is viewed by others. If interacting well is something you pray about, your children will know you put a high value on it.

2. Be Mindful of Your Nonverbal Communication

Be aware of your body language, tone of voice, and facial expressions—they influence your children's opinion of others and themselves.

Beware of multitasking! When our attention is already divided between texting a coworker and folding the laundry, we can't respond to our children with the attention they deserve. Multitasking breaks down our focus, and that breaks down our manners.

Think about other nonverbal messages and attitudes you model for your children on a daily basis.

- How do you respond to the nightly news?

- Do you speak respectfully about those in public office even if they are not the candidates you voted for?

- What do you say and what's your demeanor when you hang up the phone after talking to your mom, your mother-in-law, your boss, or your neighbor?

- How do you treat waiters and interact with cashiers? Is it the way you would want people to treat your children if they held either of those jobs?

Children are mimics. They're going to act like us even if we to try teach them not to.

3. Teach Nicely and Apologize as Needed

I've overheard frazzled moms say, "You're driving me crazy! Stop it—you're being a brat." In fact, I've been one of those moms. Our calling and responsibility as parents is to be the bigger person in the truest sense of the word. Yelling, demanding, showing frustration, and name-calling don't exactly model kind, Christlike manners.

Children will be children. We need a double dose of patience to deal with them on some days. On the days when you don't have it, be honest and open, and ask your child nicely for help. "Honey, I'm not myself today. Would you help me by not asking for anything else in the store? We came here to pick up three things, and I'd like to get those things and go home." This acknowledges your feelings and models a kinder and more reasonable response, one you'd like them to use when they're frustrated.

For those days when we don't have a double dose of patience and we react in a way that we regret, the best thing we can do is admit our failure and sincerely ask our children for forgiveness. This allows our children to see what it looks like to fail and to humbly own up to it and seek forgiveness.

I keep the problems of the adult world to myself, but I share about my shortcomings with my children, and I apologize when I'm wrong.

I was angry and yelled at you when I saw that you didn't clean your room after I asked you to do it this morning. I expect you to do what I ask you to do, but I was wrong to yell. I was also wrong to do it in front of your brother instead of speaking to you alone. I'm going to try to not raise my voice to you. Will you please forgive me? Now, what if I help get you started by working with you for the first ten minutes?

Apologizing shows that you respect yourself and your child.

4. Be Gradual

We're sometimes so eager to change the atmosphere in our homes that we're tempted to say, "Listen up everyone. Changes are coming! I've learned some great new things, and we're going to start walking in graciousness around here! Here's a list of twenty-five manners that I want all of us to use. Let's get started! There will be a new list next week."

If you bombard your children with too many new things, they'll feel overwhelmed. You might even find them giving up before they ever really get started. In addition, the constant reminders you would have to give them would quickly morph into nagging.

A different approach is to prayerfully consider what area of manners you want to begin working on first (conversations, kind words, dining, first impressions, and such). Then pick out the top three manners in that area. When your child gets those three right about half the time, add on two or three more skills. In this way she will make slow but steady and sure progress.

5. Brief and Debrief

In college and through my twenties I worked in retail management. Every few years a vice president from the home office would visit. These were important meetings, and I never went into one without having been thoroughly prepared by my regional manager. These briefings were important to my success.

Just as my regional manager prepared me for successful meetings, children must be trained in social skills. This is part of the *work* of growing up.

Knowing what to say and how to act in Sunday school, at a birthday party, during a playdate, or on a first date does not come naturally. It's not common sense; it's uncommon sense.

An eight-year-old can't surmise on her own that she should thank Mrs. Monroe for dinner when the chicken casserole had "yucky" green vegetables in it. Our 17-year-old can't see any reason to go to the front door and introduce himself to Rachel's parents when he picks her up for a date. After all, it's easier if he just shoots her a text from the driveway: "I'm here."

When we know that an upcoming event will challenge our children's social skills, we can take advantage of two teaching opportunities: briefing before the event and debriefing after the event.

Think about things that might occur at an upcoming event and then talk about or role-play them with your children so they're prepared in advance. Knowledge brings confidence. You'll equip them to be more at ease, other centered, and well received.

After the event, you can debrief them even if you weren't with them. Ask questions: "What did you have for dinner?" "What did you say when you thanked Mrs. Monroe? I bet she liked being appreciated."

When your daughter tells you she didn't thank Mrs. Monroe or your son says he didn't meet Rachel's parents, there's no reason to correct them immediately. Make a mental note and before the next event, brief them about what to do. "Sweetie, I know you don't like green vegetables. You don't need to thank her for the vegetables. However, Mrs. Monroe is kind to invite you to eat with them. Tell her 'thank you' for dinner." To your son you might say, "Introduce yourself to Rachel's parents. It's the right thing to do, and they'll feel more comfortable letting Rachel go out with you after meeting you."

Brief and debrief, and you'll be able to prepare your children and then catch them being kind and mannerly. What you catch, you can encourage!

Our children can't read our minds. We need to explain the connection between our thoughts and our actions. Children need to understand that manners start with kind thoughts that are then translated into kind words and actions. For example, you might explain to your daughter,

"Bailey, I wanted to do something special for you today, so I made you brownies with peanut butter fudge frosting. I know they're your favorite!" Now Bailey understands the kind thought behind your kind action of making brownies.

6. Notice and Praise

Children tend to give us more of what we notice. If we notice our children being mannerly and compliment them on it, they'll strive to please us by doing it again. We all enjoy hearing, "Great job!" The more you can say it, the more you'll enjoy the fruits of their good manners.

We can not only compliment our children on good behavior but also compliment them when they stop a poor behavior. "Jackson, I've noticed that you've been kind to your little sister. You've not called her any names. You helped her pick up the toys in the family room after lunch, and you offered to pour her some juice when I was on the phone with Grandma. You're really growing in patience and kindness! I notice, and I'm proud of you!"

Noticing and praising can have a downside. If done for every little thing, they can turn our children into praise addicts. In order to keep your efforts from backfiring, offer specific praise.

It's better to praise specific acts than just your child's good manners in general. Saying, "I appreciate your good manners today, Joshua!" is nice, but it's not going to directly impact his future actions as much as specific praise will. With generic praise a child is never totally sure of what he did or didn't do that constituted his good manners. You said his manners were good, so it must be okay that during his playdate with Ian today he rather rudely told Ian's little brother, "Go play by yourself." He also jumped on their family room sofa, and when he got hungry he helped himself to two snack packs of Doritos without asking.

On the other hand, praise for something more specific paints a clear picture for him, and he's likely to repeat the manners you mention again. "Joshua, I noticed how you said, 'Good morning, Mrs. Koenig' when she opened the door and how you thanked her for the cookies when she offered them to you. You even threw your napkin away when you were done eating. Those were kind and thoughtful actions. I'm really impressed, and Mrs. Koenig told me she was too!"

Another effective way to take notice and give praise is to comment on the actions of others. As you watch TV together, talk with your child about the words and actions of the people they see. Ask if they believe the people acted kindly and how they could have handled situations differently. If a clerk at the grocery store is especially friendly and helpful, comment to your child about how nice that makes people feel.

There is one pitfall you'll want to avoid as you take notice and give praise. It's labeling. "I'm sorry, Savannah doesn't talk much. She's my quiet child." "I'm sorry that Rebecca is playing so rough. She's my little rebel." One thing is practically certain: Savannah and Rebecca will grow into those labels until they fit too snugly to take off.

Even a good label can become cumbersome. Growing up feeling as if your place in life is to always be good, smart, responsible, and so on is like wearing a crown that eventually digs uncomfortably into your head.

Also, watch out for giving negative labels to your children's feelings: "You always get so angry," or "You're always quick to judge," or "You get worked up too easily." Saying these things makes our children feel as if their emotions control them.

Let your children know that they have power over their emotions. "You seem worked up this evening. Let's talk about your anger. I know you'll figure out how to work through it."

7. Follow the 80–20 Rule

It's easier to notice the negative than the positive. Studies show that 96 percent of the messages most people deliver to their children are negative, including...

corrections	negative facial expressions
threats	
raised voices	being unavailable, uninterested, or rushed
anger	

If 96 percent of messages are negative, that means only 4 percent are positive. These rare positive interactions include...

hugs and kisses	reading
compliments	talking
listening nonjudg-	laughing
mentally	relaxing
playing	working side by side

We hope that our homes are not 96 percent negative and only 4 percent positive. But in reality, we are probably more negative than we realize, and this will hinder our children in their adult relationships.

The ideal ratio to nurture a strong, trusting, and respectful bond between a parent and child is 80 percent positive and 20 percent negative. This kind of change in communication will take effort on our part, especially when there are socks on the floor, dirty plates on the coffee table, and garbage spilling out of the trash can because the teenager didn't take it out![1]

The most powerful kind of positive communication you can give your child is to simply say, "I love you"—spontaneously and affectionately. Try this one day: Stop what you're doing, go to where your son is, sit down, look him in the eyes, and say, "I was in the other room thinking about you. You are special and dear. I love being your mom, and I love you. I love who you are and who you're becoming. Always remember that, okay?"

Your child might be shy or stunned, but he will remember what you said, and that's what's important. The only power we have to influence our children's hearts is what they give us freely through love. Our children will be more in tune with from-the-heart interactions if we spontaneously and affectionately show our love for them by saying "I love you!" or "I'm so glad I'm your mom!" or "You mean the world to me" every day.

If the heart connection isn't there, you might still have an obedient child, but the obedience will only control her actions. How much better for your child to want to do the act in kindness, for her heart to be in it. Obedience can flow out of fear or respect. Your goal is respect—obedience born from love.

8. Require

Children who have good manners have parents who require it. Make obtaining them a nonnegotiable in your home. Not every little rule and nuance, of course, but insist on the heart of manners, of purposefully inter-acting with care and thoughtfulness in your interactions. I pray for manners to be a hallmark of our home. Kent and I share stories with the boys about our ancestors who loved the Lord and accomplished much because of their ability to grow in favor with God and man.

Good manners are keys to getting along well with others in this time and place Christ has placed us in. Proverbs 22:6 says, "Point your kids in the right direction—when they're old they won't be lost." Good manners are more than just social niceties; they are core ingredients in a harmonious family, a peaceful community, and a civilized republic.

Having said that, I don't want you to scan through this book, see the lists of manners, and think, "That Maralee! She seems really nice, but she's crazy if she thinks any child can learn all this stuff!"

Please hear my heart. I'm not suggesting that your children will learn everything in this book. They probably won't. They definitely won't learn it all at once. They won't even learn it all in the next five years. Some of it won't matter to you, and you'll never tell them about those parts.

And you know what? That's okay! What matters is that you have all the tools you need to provide your children with the information they need for their relationships to thrive when they're grown.

Fifty Years from Now

Half a century from today, the oak tree in my backyard and I will probably be gone. But Lord willing, my children will still be going strong.

Whom will God be blessing through them? I often ponder this question. It helps me get through some of the tougher days when my boys' wills clash with the rules and manners my husband and I have set up. We created this framework to nurture their character, strengthen ours, and better prepare each of us to represent Christ in our interactions.

Along with prayers, it takes daily watering, careful watching, and delicate pruning to raise children who are growing in graciousness. Oh, how it's worth all the work! The seedlings you and I nourish today will offer the wide welcome and sheltering care of Christ to their generation and beyond.

4

The Five-Star First Impression

*Whatever makes an impression on
the heart seems lovely in the eye.*

Sa'Di

Etiquette IQ Quiz

Take this brief quiz to get a taste of what you'll learn from this chapter.

1. When you meet someone for the first time, how long does it take for him to form a lasting impression of you?

   A. twenty seconds or less

   B. one minute

   C. three minutes

2. When shaking hands, what's the correct number of times to pump the other person's hand up and down?

   A. three times

   B. four times

   C. five times

3. When meeting or greeting someone, when do girls and ladies stand?

   A. only to greet other girls and ladies

   B. to greet everyone

   C. In social settings girls and ladies remain seated; in business settings ladies stand to greet everyone.*

*Answers: 1) A 2) A 3) B.

37

"He's here, Maralee!" the doctor exclaimed with a mixture of relief and excitement.

Immediately, I reached out my arms for my baby.

Even before the cord was cut, I was holding him, his fists clenched and eyes closed. I ever so gently rubbed my cheek against the velveteen hairs of his head. I felt bliss. My eyes watered in wonderment. My husband and I beamed at him, hugged him, and whispered to him that he was loved and special and a joy.

As I continued to talk to him, his eyes opened. They were as clear as two perfect diamonds, almost as big as his newborn fists, and as blue as the Caribbean sky. A few minutes into our bonding the most heavenly thing happened: His clenched fists uncurled. I gently placed my trembling pinkie into his delicate, open palm, and he instinctively squeezed my finger.

Marc Robert McKee was only three minutes old, yet I had been able to communicate to him that he was wanted and welcomed. Now, 15 years later, he's six feet two, yet I still express my tenderness for him in pretty much the same way: a heartfelt smile, my complete attention, a touch, gentle words, and a gaze into his eyes.

We never outgrow our craving to reexperience our delivery-room welcome. It's the simple gift of attention expressed as a look, a smile, a touch, and special words. When people purposefully meet or greet us in this way, they fill our human need to feel noticed, esteemed, and welcomed. In response, people are drawn to us as naturally as the compass is drawn to true north.

As we teach our children to warmly welcome others and explain how they can encourage people to instinctively uncurl their fists and let go of cynicism and self-centeredness, we give them the tools to earn respect, trust, and friendship.

First Greetings and Lasting Impressions

We've all heard that first impressions matter, but few of us realize how much a first impression determines whether someone will view us favorably. If we did, the little-known and easy-to-learn formula I'm about to share with you would be taught to children as diligently as the ABCs or multi-plication tables.

This is the manners skill set I most want my sons and students to fully understand and embrace because positive first impressions are the corner-stone of forming positive relationships. First impressions inevitably set the tone for how others perceive, interact, and respond to you.

Studies from before the 1950s have shown that in about seven sec-onds—the time it takes our eyes to scan someone from head to toe—we form an opinion about him.[1] We sum up, rightly or wrongly, his likeability, level of education, moral code, socioeconomic status, and more.

Have you ever been waiting in your car at a red light, noticed some-one on the sidewalk, and checked to make sure your doors were locked? If so, you're like me, and we've just proved how quickly we get a feeling about people. A quick judgment like this isn't always bad. It may help us avoid a dangerous situation.

On the other hand, what if a first impression is inaccurate? We all like to think we're good judges of character, so we're slow to change our first impressions. In fact, before we can convince ourselves that an initial impression of someone was incorrect, we need multiple additional interac-tions with her. The number depends on the type of interactions—face-to-face meetings, phone calls, e-mails, text messages, and so on.

To keep our opinion of a person in line with our first impression, we'll ignore or rationalize discrepancies. For example, we might overhear a new acquaintance make demeaning remarks to her children and think, "When I met her I could tell she was actually a sweet person, so she must be hav-ing a stressful day." This impression about a person is what psychologists call our *retained remembrance*. We maintain one for everyone we encounter, and we form it during those critical first seven to ten seconds. We don't like to admit we were wrong. We're more inclined to defend our initial reaction: "I knew the first time I saw her that she had a giving spirit," or "I knew the moment I met her new boyfriend, he wasn't the faithful type."

The Formula for Five-Star First Impressions

In the first ten seconds of meeting and greeting someone, you can offer him the gift of you at your best.

I've taught the Five-Star First Impression formula to several thousand children and probably as many adults. It's the same whether we're nine or forty-nine. Teach it to your children now, and they'll benefit throughout their lives.

The formula contains the things we can do and the words we can say to help us make our best impression. In addition, the formula also gives us an excellent structure for greeting anyone—not just new acquaintances. Using it to greet relatives and friends we don't see regularly will help us quickly reconnect our hearts with theirs. Here are the five steps, followed by tips for making each one a natural part of your child's life.

1. Stand up.
2. Smile big.
3. See the other person.
4. Shake hands.
5. Say the perfect welcome.

   Share a nice greeting.

   Say the other person's name.

   Add a thank-you, a sincere compliment, or a well-wish.

1. Stand Up

You have just ten seconds to make your first impression, so start to stand up as soon as you see the other person approaching. Standing is a sign of respect and glad anticipation. It signals the person that you're rising to the occasion of meeting or greeting her. Standing also shows that you're going to stop whatever you were doing and give her your undivided attention. It's the first nonverbal invitation you send to her. "Come on over! I'm glad you're here!"

Good posture makes a difference at this moment. Children are wigglers, and teens tend to lean on something or slouch. For these brief ten seconds, stand straight and tall but naturally and not in a forced manner. There's no need to look like a guard at Buckingham Palace.

The best place for hands is at your side. When nervous, boys tend to put their hands in their pockets and girls often put theirs behind their backs. Instead, your arms should be at your side so you are ready to offer a handshake.

Finally, at any age, nothing will burst a first impression like chewing on gum or blowing a bubble. Keep your gum under your tongue while meeting and greeting others.

Growing in Graciousness
(Next-Level Skills)

Standing and Greeting

After your child consistently remembers to stand up when meeting and greeting, teach the following skills.

Step around any physical barriers between you and the other person. Greeting someone from across a dining table or while standing on the other side of a desk or coffee table sends a verbal message that you want to keep some distance between you and the other person. Whenever it's possible for you to move without disturbing others near you, make sure nothing but air separates you and the other person.

Whenever you're not able to stand up, offer an apology. Perhaps you cannot stand because the person sitting beside you in your booth at a restaurant doesn't know to stand to meet a new person. In that case, offer a quick apology in your greeting. "I'm sorry for not standing." This will let the person you're meeting know you wanted to be respectful and stand but couldn't.

We all stand for everyone. Generations past held to all kinds of rules about when and for whom girls and ladies would stand. Now, out of equal respect for each other regardless of our age or gender, it's considered polite to stand to greet one another.

2. Smile Big

A smile is your nonverbal invitation for the person to join you. Before you say your first word, your smile signals to the other person that you're happy to see him. Don't be afraid of a big smile. Let your pearly whites convey from across the room that you welcome his company. Comedian and pianist Victor Borge wisely said, "The shortest distance between two people is a smile."

3. See the Other Person

Our eyes are the windows to our souls. If we want to make a great impression, we must literally see eye to eye. For the first ten seconds of meeting or greeting someone, let her be your sole focus. Your eyes will portray what your heart feels: "I'm glad you're here!"

Making eye contact can be a challenge for children and adults, but some simple tricks make it much easier.

Use the spy spot to overcome shyness. If it is stressful to look into another person's eyes, you can look at the spy spot instead. To locate the spy spot, envision a circle right above the bridge of the other person's nose. If you look into that spot while talking to her, she'll never know you're not looking right into her eyes. I call it the spy spot because it's an old trick spies used to help them disseminate misinformation without batting an eye. You can use the spy spot to make this step fun for your child. You can whisper in his ear, "Honey, remember to look at Mrs. Gibson's spy spot when you say hello," and he will look forward to trying his new game. In time, just as he grows out of training wheels, he won't need this mental device to be able to confidently and graciously look others in the eyes.

Encourage your children to make eye contact with anyone who speaks to them. We've all talked to someone who has been texting, watching TV, reading a magazine, or doing a million things other than looking at us. It's frustrating! You never know how much, if any, of what you're saying they're taking in. People don't know you care about them or their concerns until they see it in your eyes.

Can you tell me what color eyes she had? Look in the other person's eyes long enough to make a mental note of her eye color. This causes you to really focus on her. In doing so, you'll convey welcome, care, interest, and trust with your eyes.

4. Shake Hands

Your handshake is your personal seal of approval. People shake hands to declare good intentions toward each other through a physical connection. Too often we're unsure whether a handshake is appropriate, so we don't offer our hand. However, handshakes are almost always welcomed, especially if done correctly.

A great handshake makes for a great impression, but a weak or poor one sends a signal that even your smile, eye contact, or words might not overcome. Everyone has experienced a weak handshake when the person barely made contact with your hand and left you wondering, "Did she not want to touch me?" Then there's the handshake that is so strong it hurts and turns your smile into a grimace. The perfect handshake is what I call the Thumbs-Up Handshake. Children and adults alike love learning about it in the classes I teach. Here are the three easy steps.

1. Make the thumbs-up sign with your right hand. Keeping your thumb up, open your hand and point your fingers straight out in front of you. Keep your fingers next to each other and not spread apart. You want the skin between your thumb and first

(pointer) finger touching the same spot on the other person's hand.

2. Extend your hand toward the other person until the base of your thumb touches the base of his thumb and let your fingers curve gently around each other's hands.

3. Shake, or "pump," the other person's hand up and down three times and then uncurl your fingers from around his hand to end the handshake.

That's all there is to having a handshake that fully connects you to the other person!

ℳom to ℳom

The Evolving Etiquette of Handshakes

The rules of the past generation for who should extend his hand first are fading fast. I teach my own children and those in all my classes to extend a hand to anyone they meet. By the time they're grown, it will be the prevailing etiquette of the times. As it is today, a man no longer needs to wait for a woman to extend her hand, and children may extend their hands to adults. (This not the case in other countries, so check local customs when traveling or entertaining foreign guests.)

Fist bumps, starbursts, high fives, and other alternative forms of handshaking are fine ways for children and teens to greet their peers. However, when meeting adults, children and teens should extend their hands for a traditional handshake.

If you shook someone's hand when you said hello, it's nice to shake hands again when you say goodbye.

5. Say the Perfect Welcome

The first four parts of our Five-Star First Impression formula deal with the things we do when we're meeting or greeting someone: stand up, smile, look into the other person's eyes, and shake her hand. The final ingredient in our formula shows us how to say words that are as impressive and other-centered as our actions.

Learning to say the perfect welcome has had more of an impact on my self-confidence and poise than any other etiquette skill set. It's such a relief not to have to think about what I'm going to say or worry that I'll accidently say the wrong thing. I didn't learn how to say the perfect welcome until I was 33, but I've already taught it to both my sons. It's a joy to see them meet others with ease and present their best selves to the world. If I had learned this simple etiquette 20 years earlier, I would have been more confident about the way others viewed me, and I could have formed relationships more easily.

The perfect welcome has three parts. When you put the three parts together, you'll have about ten words. That's one word for each second of our first impression. Of course, there's no need to count your words. Seven words, ten, fifteen…you get the idea. It's all fine. Having a ten-word goal simply gives our children an easy target.

1. Share a nice greeting. Simply saying hello is a nice way to meet or greet someone. However, remember that there are other greetings too. Referring to the time of day ("Good morning") is always nice. Whenever you are greeting near a holiday or a special occasion, it's wonderful to replace the standard hello with something more specific, such as "Merry Christmas" or "Happy birthday."

2. Say the other person's name. Do you want to know what everyone's favorite word is? It's his or her name, so use it often! Of course, you won't always know the name of the other person (we'll look at what to do in that case in the next chapter), but if you do, say it after your initial greeting. "Good afternoon, Mrs. Lopez," or "Happy birthday, Uncle Keith."

3. Add a thank-you, a sincere compliment, or a well-wish. This step gives us the opportunity to express a heart full of gratitude. First, give your initial greeting, referring to the time or occasion as specifically as possible. For example, "Happy birthday, Layla!" Then add your appreciation: "Thank you for inviting me to your party!" or "Good afternoon, Mrs. Crosby. Thank you for tutoring me." If you're greeting someone you already know, a well-wish is always a thoughtful add-on. A well-wish is simply saying that you wish for something to go well for the person. "Good morning, Mrs. Abelson. I hope you have a great day."

Of course, as in all etiquette teaching, the rules don't change based on our age. The same formula works perfectly for us as well as our children. We moms can say, "Good afternoon, Mr. Dodd. Thank you for returning my call," or "Happy anniversary, Shanna. I'm so happy for you."

This third part of the perfect welcome requires some advanced skills. You can add it to the mix after your child or teen has mastered the first two parts. Greeting someone with his or her name and a sincere sentiment requires some thought, but the results are well worth the effort. When we use these skills, we'll always hit the perfect note.

How Skills Work with Different Personalities

Here is how these skills have worked with my two sons, who are greatly different in age and in personality.

Marc, my oldest, is an introvert and relies on the Five-Star First Impression formula as a safety net for meeting and greeting. He has been complimented by strangers in line at the grocery store, sales clerks, restaurant servers, and even by a US representative at a fund-raiser he attended with his grandmother. Every compliment and positive encounter is a notch in his belt of social success, giving this introvert and perfectionist the courage he needs to feel comfortable interacting with others.

Corbett, my youngest, is our family's extrovert. He also has a mild degree of ADHD. The Five-Star First Impression formula has given him clear-cut boundaries, helping him to know when he's spoken enough. Like his big brother, he also receives compliments from strangers and friends. The positive encounters he has experienced have given him the healthiest type of self-esteem—the kind that is reflected back to him because of the kindness he has extended to others.

The Warmest Welcome

As moms, we'll never forget the delivery-room welcome we gave our children. It was filled with tenderness, attention, and joy. When we use the skills in this chapter to honor others and lift them up, we go beyond merely meeting or interacting with people—we connect with them. And when we make people feel special, something marvelous occurs: They think we're pretty special too. We are drawn into a Christ-honoring circle of mutual respect and caring.

Inspiration and Application

1. In Philippians 1:1-3 (NIV), Paul greets the recipients of his letter: "To all God's holy people in Christ Jesus at Philippi, together with the overseers and deacons: Grace and peace to you from God our Father and the Lord Jesus Christ. I thank my God every time I remember you." What are the similarities between Paul's greeting and the three parts of the perfect welcome that we just discovered? If Paul were alive today and greeting the Philippians on Skype, what might he say as he appeared on the church's large-screen monitor?

2. Proverbs 30:32-33 says, "If you're dumb enough to call attention to yourself by offending people and making rude gestures, don't be surprised if someone bloodies your nose. Churned milk turns into butter; riled emotions turn into fist fights." Our words and gestures affect others' emotions. What are a couple of the benefits we give our children and teens when we teach them to be purposeful in the way they meet and greet others and give them the tools to do it?

3. To test your memory, try listing the five parts of our formula for a Five-Star First Impression.

4. When our children are too nervous to look someone in the eyes, they can focus on a particular spot on her face and appear to be

looking her in the eyes. This technique is a first step toward getting comfortable with the important and respectful act of looking others in the eyes. What did we call the special spot they can focus on, and where is it located?

5. What name did we use for the perfect handshake? List the three steps of the handshake using the words you'll use when you teach it to your child.

5

How Do You Do Your "How-Do-You-Do's"?

*The very essence of politeness [is] to take care
that by our words and actions we make other people
pleased with us as well as with themselves.*
JEAN DE LA BRUYÈRE

Etiquette IQ Quiz

1. Your child does not need to introduce himself to...

   A. a guest in your home who is visiting someone else in the family

   B. a friend's family members at the friend's house

   C. someone who stops to talk to a person you're with

2. What's the kindest thing to do if you forget the name of the person you're conversing with?

   A. Don't use his name in conversation. This way you won't draw attention to the fact that you can't remember it.

   B. Say, "Please forgive me. I'm having a brain lapse, and I can't recall your name."

   C. Say, "Please tell me your name again."

3. When you are introducing yourself, which name should you say?

   A. your full given name: "Beth Ann Horn"

   B. both your full given name and the name you like to be called if it's different from your first name: "Beth Ann Horn, but everyone calls me Beth"

C. the name you want the other person to call you by and your last name: "Beth Horn"*

There's nothing like hearing the sound of your name to make you feel welcomed and wanted. In fact, studies show that the first word babies recognize is their own name. At about 16 weeks old, when a baby hears her name, she'll turn in the direction of the person who said it whether that person is a family member or stranger.[1]

This instinct is both precious and revealing. It shows that the first password to our heart is our name. That's why it's so important that our children are comfortable with the skill of introducing themselves and others. Introduction skills enable us and our children to help others feel welcome and important.

In my private coaching sessions and corporate seminars, many adults have told me they are hesitant to make introductions because they've heard there are a lot of rules about whose name to say first, what phrasing to use, and such. Unsure of the myriad of guidelines, they choose not to make introductions rather than risk getting them wrong.

Let me set your mind at ease. Introductions don't have to be that complicated! I've reduced the pages of protocols into simple formulas of just three steps each. This makes them easy enough for children to learn (in stages), yet they're no different from what I teach adults. It's nice to know that our children, tweens, and teens can learn them now and rely on them confidently for life.

Where Everybody Knows Your Name

Do you remember the television show *Cheers*? It ran from 1982 to 1993. The title of its theme song always stood out to me: "Where Everybody Knows Your Name."

In the television show, the regulars showed up in the Cheers pub because they felt welcomed and included there. At Cheers they were *known*. The gang at Cheers was on to something when they all called out, "Norm!" every time he stepped in the door.

---

* Answers: 1) C 2) C 3) C.

The truth is, we all long to belong. You probably don't remember each time you've been part of a group, but I bet (like me) you can recount almost every time you've felt left out, isolated, or ignored. Introductions are the first defense against exclusion.

When we skip introducing ourselves or others, we miss opportunities to form relationships. We can be mistaken for being aloof, and people needing to be introduced may feel excluded or even invisible. However, when we're confident with our introductions, we reflect thoughtfulness and respect. Sharing your name is the first personal gift you give someone. It says, "Here's something about me that I'd like you to know." Introductions are the first step in transitioning from being strangers to being known.

Just Do It!

When we initially begin making introductions, they can seem awkward—even difficult. Most people need to make several introductions in different social settings before they feel comfortable. But as Matthew 5:47 shares, "If you simply say hello to those who greet you, do you expect a medal? Any run-of-the-mill sinner does that." Knowing this, let's go the extra mile to introduce ourselves and others so our children will learn the gift of including others.

If you find yourself unsure of the right way to make an introduction, make it anyway. People often ask me, "Maralee, what should I do when I'm not certain of exactly how to make an introduction?" My answer, "Smile, speak kindly and confidently, and do it!" Friendliness and inclusion are always better than ignoring someone because of uncertainty.

The formulas you're about to read are perfect for family, business, and social use. The only rare exceptions are some diplomatic, military, or very formal events. (If you need to prepare for one of these, you'll want to consult a book of diplomatic protocols from your local library or search online for "Diplomatic Introductions.")

Let's get started by looking at the basic wrapping we need to put on all our introductions.

Basic Instructions for All Introductions

During an introduction, you're giving another person the gift of a name and a potential relationship. As with any present, small details make a big impact. Is the gift wrapped nicely? Is there a pretty bow on the box? Is the card signed and attached? That's why we wrap our introductions in the expression of welcome we learned through the Five-Star First Impression formula.

1. Stand up.

2. Smile big.

3. See the other person (by making eye contact).

4. Shake hands.

As you may remember, the Five-Star First Impression formula has five steps. When you're making a first impression, your fifth step is to say the perfect welcome. When you're making an introduction, your fifth step will include the words of the perfect introduction.

The rest of this chapter will look at various formulas for the different kinds of introductions. You'll find out how to introduce yourself with ease and poise and how to respond with friendliness to introductions from others.

You'll also learn how to use *sir*, *ma'am*, and other titles and honorifics in a way that makes sense today. Let's start by learning what to say when we introduce ourselves.

How to Introduce Yourself—the Formula

After you have established your positive first impression (stand up, smile big, see the other person by making eye contact, and shake hands), you are ready to make the perfect introduction of yourself. Here's the formula.

1. *Share a nice greeting.* "Hi" or "hey" isn't up to par with the level of greeting you want to give. "Hello!" is fine. Even better is a two-word greeting—something like, "Good morning," or "Merry Christmas."

2. *Share your first and last names.* There are lots of Abigails, Zoes, Aarons, and Zacks in the world. Make yourself known (if safety isn't an issue) by using your first and last names. "Good afternoon. I'm Zoe Barton."

3. *Say, "It's nice to meet you!"* Yes, this is a scripted phrase. But trust me, it always works. Just memorize it, and you'll always know the perfect thing to say after you introduce yourself.

Teach your children to introduce themselves to others with the name they want to be called. If Jonathan Shane Thompson wants to be called Shane instead of Jonathan or Jon, he should introduce himself as Shane Thompson. Katherine Rose Johnson should introduce herself as Katy Johnson if that's the name she currently prefers. Often young children with their high sense of wanting to be truthful (a good thing!) will share lengthy stories regarding their names. Teach children that they can share their name without feeling as if they need to explain.

If your child is shy and hesitant to make introductions, tell him that the payoffs are more than worth the momentary stress. By the simple fact that you introduce yourself first, you're seen as outgoing, friendly, and approachable. People look for and admire these traits.

Unless you're just casually passing by someone, it's usually best to introduce yourself. Here are some people to whom you should always introduce yourself:

- guests in your home, even if they're visiting with someone else in your family

- other guests at parties you attend, especially at someone's home

- teachers and classmates

- anyone who is new to your school club, sports team, Sunday school class, and so on

- anyone who is in the house when you're visiting a friend at his or her home

Introductions are almost always appropriate because they are so brief. An introduction is the preface to the conversation. Keep your introduction short and casual so you can move quickly into conversation. In general, after you share, the other person will naturally begin to talk without you having to ask him or her to do so.

Do you ever have a hard time understanding someone's name when you first hear it? When we say our names quickly, the other person often wonders whether she heard us correctly. This puts her in the spot of having to admit she didn't hear us. Many people are reluctant to ask for a name again, so they simply won't use it, which slows down feeling comfortable with one another. You can help avoid this problem by using your first name twice in your introduction. "Good evening. I'm Debbie—Debbie Poulalion."

Both moms and children sometimes need to introduce themselves to an entire group. For example, children often are asked to introduce themselves to the class on the first day of school. Moms are asked to introduce themselves at Bible studies, parties, and other events.

For these times it's nice to have three things about yourself that you are ready to share anytime you might need to introduce yourself to a group. Sometimes the group leader gives guidelines about what to share: "Tell the group your name and your favorite flavor of ice cream." But if there are no guidelines, share your name and the three brief things that you planned in advance. Here's a "mom" example: "Good morning, everyone! I'm Tia—Tia Friedman. I have a daughter who is almost two, and I enjoy running and yoga." Children would say something like, "Hello! I'm Jayden—Jayden Larks. I have a little sister and two dogs, and I'm on a Pop Warner football team."

Growing in Graciousness
(Next-Level Skills)

Self-Introductions

You may pause conversation in order to introduce yourself. Even if a conversation has gone on for several minutes, it's

fine to stop what you are saying and introduce yourself. "...
So that's how we ended up at this church. I apologize—we
don't know each other's names. Good evening! I'm Maralee—Maralee McKee." (As you say this you would be smiling,
looking in the person's eyes, and shaking hands.) Be sure to
interrupt the conversation while you are talking, not while the
other person is talking!

How to Respond to Introductions—the Formula

Now that we've learned the perfect introduction for ourselves, we need
to make sure we have the perfect response for an introduction from someone else. Keep in mind that when someone introduces herself, she's giving
you the gift of her name. The natural response is to acknowledge the gift
and give your name in return.

Imagine that Angela has
introduced herself to you by
saying, "Good afternoon! I'm
Angela—Angela Hull! It's
nice to meet you!" Before you
say anything, give the nonverbal responses from the Five-
Star First Impression (stand
up, smile big, see the other
person by making eye con-
tact, and shake hands). Then
you can put together your
verbal response using this
three-step formula.

1. Greet her by name.
   "Good afternoon,
   Angela!"

2. Share your first and

Mom to Mom

When you introduce yourself to a
group, it's best to tell things about
yourself that will establish common ground with your audience.
Relationships build from common
ground. Don't strive to impress. It's
better to share that you have two
children and enjoy photography and
blogging than to say you were Miss
Michigan in 2002 or went to Harvard. Including your accomplishments in an introduction seems more
like bragging than sharing. If a relationship blooms into friendship, you
would certainly share more complete
information about your life.

last name, giving your first name twice. "I'm Sherrie—Sherrie Purvis."

3. Say, "It's very nice to meet you," and use the other person's name again. "It's very nice to meet you, Angela!"

Growing in Graciousness
(Next-Level Skills)

Elusive Names

Names are elusive. It seems that when you most want to know a name, it's just not there. Here is what to do when these situations arise.

What if the other person doesn't share his name? Many people aren't aware of how to introduce themselves or respond to an introduction. I have often introduced myself to people who smiled, said hello, and shook my hand but never said their name. When this happens I say in a pleasant, conversational tone, "Please tell me your name." I've never had anyone not happily share it. After the other person tells you her name, you can use it right away by saying, "Thank you, Martha. It's nice to meet you."

What if you forget someone's name? It happens to everyone, so don't worry. And don't take it too personally if someone forgets your name. This may feel counterintuitive, but it's best not to apologize when you forget someone's name. Simply and nicely ask her to repeat her name: "Please tell me your name again." After she responds, say "thank you" and repeat her name back. "Thank you, Martha." Apologizing might seem like the nice thing to do, but it actually draws more attention to the fact that you forgot her name.

"Yes, Sir" and "No, Ma'am"

The Woodstock generation taught our parents or grandparents not to trust anyone more than 30 years old. That's laughable to us now, but it ushered in a youth-obsessed culture that wants to stay young in looks and attitude—forever. People get Botox injections at 33 and face-lifts at 41, and today's 67-year-old grandmas are as likely to be at a health spa as a quilting bee. Looking good and staying in shape is great, and based on my reflection in the mirror lately, I wouldn't mind looking ten years younger than I am.

There isn't a problem with wanting to stay youthful. But a problem arises when a young person honors someone as an elder and that elder is insulted by the truth behind the courtesy. It happens in many settings. For example, when well-meaning receptionists, sales clerks, or servers address customers respectfully with "sir" or "ma'am," they are often rebuked. Being elders doesn't mean we're ancient. It only means we're adults. If a waiter asks me a question, even though he might be ten years younger than me, I might still reply with a warm "Yes, sir." It's a respectful way to respond, especially if you don't know a person's last name and can't use the norm of the business world, which would be to say his last name: "Thank you for returning my phone call, Mr. Rollins."

Courtesy titles are even being rejected in the classroom. One of my sons answered his teacher by saying, "Yes, ma'am," and she rebuked him

> ### *Mom to Mom*
>
> What do you do if someone is addressing you or your child by the wrong name? If you're talking to him in passing, there's no need to correct him. If you're having a lengthy conversation, or you're at a small party or event, or if you think you'll meet him again, it's best to correct the mistake—and soon. The longer you let it go on, the more times he may say your name incorrectly, and the more embarrassed he'll be when he realizes his mistake. (I know this from experience!) It's pretty simple to correct. Just graciously say something like this: "Actually, I prefer Kathleen," or "His name is Jake, not Jack. The two names do sound alike though."

in front of the class. She said, "You're a new student, so I'll let it slide this one time. Don't call me 'ma'am.' I don't like it." Embarrassed and unsure of what to say, he simply replied, "I'm sorry." He told me he almost accidently replied, "I'm sorry, ma'am." I wonder what would have happened then!

I've worked diligently to make using these terms of respect a habit for him—and they were until her rebuke. Since then he's been hesitant to use them. When I asked him why, he said, "Mom, what if the next woman or man doesn't like it either, and I get in trouble again? I don't want to risk it." How sad that one person's personal preference would put a strain on a teen who wants to be respectful!

In light of society's trend, one might wonder whether we should continue to teach our children to say "sir" and "ma'am." And what about referring to adults by their honorific (Mr., Miss, Ms., or Mrs.) or title (doctor, reverend, senator, sergeant, and so on)?

My answer is yes, we should! Our children should use titles and honorifics for their elders, and so should you and I. Manners don't change with our age. What is good form for a 12-year-old is just as respectful from a 32-year-old. When any of us meet someone who is a generation older than us (in etiquette, this is 20 years, not 40) we should use her title or honorific when responding to the introduction.

When thirtysomething Allie Langston is introduced to fiftysomething Carol Perez, Allie isn't wrong to respond, "Good afternoon, Ms. Perez! It's very nice to meet you." If Ms. Perez wants Allie to call her Carol, she can say, "Call me Carol."

Sir, ma'am, titles, and honorifics are verbal recognitions of respect. You will hear *sir* and *ma'am* more in the South than other parts of the country, but not exclusively so, and for good reason. These terms help our children understand that not all people are their playmates. They give adults a degree of authority.

Miss, Mrs., Ms., and Mr.

Children can refer to their teen and young-adult sitters with the word *Miss* and a first name, such as Miss Angela or Miss Tia. The use of *Miss*, even though it's said with the sitter's first name, gives an appropriate level of respect.

Children may also refer to close family friends as *Miss* or *Mr.* and their first name (regardless of whether the person is married or not). In this case, *Miss* or *Mr.* stands in for *auntie*, *cousin*, or the like. This is especially helpful when the person knows the child from a young age. Most three-year-olds can say Miss Christy. Few can say Mrs. Mowbray.

When you have introduced your best friend to your young child as Miss Christy, that's the name the child can continue to use. If, however, your child is in second grade or older when Christy becomes your best friend, he

Mom to Mom

Ma'am is the abbreviation of the French word *madame*, which translates as "my lady" and is the feminine form of *lord*. It's the official US military title for a female officer of superior rank. In addition, it's used for addressing high-ranking female members of the government, such as a woman serving as secretary of state, speaker of the house, and so on. Current presidents are addressed as "Mr. President" or "sir." When a female holds the title of president, she will be referred to in conversation as "Madame President" or "ma'am." Just in case you're ever chatting with the Queen of England, keep in mind that you only need to refer to her as Your Majesty the first time you address her in the conversation. For the remainder of your time together, simply saying "ma'am" is perfectly proper.

should be introduced to her as Mrs. Mowbray because by then most children can remember and pronounce even tongue-twister last names such as Zarbaugh and VanderKlein.

Regarding how others address you, don't ask children to call you by your first name until you've asked their parents' permission. But if that is your preference (or you have a truly challenging last name), and if the parent gives permission, then it's fine. If the mom says, "I'm trying to teach my children verbal respect for adults by referring to them as *Mr.* or *Mrs.* I hope you'll understand," then the parent's wishes should be respected.

In conversation with your children, refer to other adults by their title or honorific and last name in order to set an example of respect. Terri might be a great friend and colleague, but refer to her as Mrs. Denton when you're talking with your husband and kids over dinner about the meeting the two of you had that morning.

An Open Door

Our name is the first word we understand as babies, and throughout our lives, sharing our name is the first step in forming relationships. When we introduce ourselves, we open the doors of welcome and inclusion for others. If we fail to introduce ourselves or don't respond when people introduce themselves to us, they can feel excluded—even invisible.

We give our children a gracious advantage when we show them at a young age how to kindly make themselves known and welcome others through the simple three-step formula for introducing themselves and the easy four-step formula for responding to introductions. These are ambassador-level skills—especially for ambassadors representing Christ—that most children can master by the time they are ten years old. The skills don't change as children grow older, so they can carry them into adulthood knowing that they are warmly welcoming others and possibly planting the seeds of friendship with every "It's nice to meet you!"

Inspiration and Application

1. Matthew 5:46-48 (AMP) says, "If you love those who love you, what reward can you have? Do not even the tax collectors do that? And if you greet only your brethren, what more than others are you doing? Do not even the Gentiles (the heathen) do that? You, therefore, must be perfect [growing into complete maturity of godliness in mind and character, having reached the proper height of virtue and integrity], as your heavenly Father is perfect." After reading these verses, what expectations do you feel the Lord has for you as His child when you (and your children) meet and greet others?

2. Philippians 4:5 (AMP) says, "Let all men know and perceive and recognize your unselfishness (your considerateness, your forbearing spirit). The Lord is near [He is coming soon]." What are some of the skills listed in this chapter that will help you act graciously so others will recognize your considerate spirit?

3. What are the three steps of introducing yourself? Where can you go this week with your children to practice and model these skills?

4. What are the three steps of responding when someone introduces herself to you? Role-play with your children the how-to's of introducing themselves as well as responding to introductions. Play dress-up with ties, sport coats, purses, hats, jewelry, and so on to make it fun!

5. When someone introduces himself to us, he gives us the gift of his name. What gift should we give him in exchange? If you introduce yourself to someone who doesn't know to offer you his name in return (you'll find this happens a lot), what should you say to him?

Turning Strangers into Friends

*The unnamed should not be
mistaken for the nonexistent.*
CATHARINE A. MACKINNON

Etiquette IQ Quiz

1. When introducing two of your friends to each other, which of the following phrases is considered best form?

   A. "I'd like you to meet…"

   B. "I'd like to introduce…"

   C. "I'd like to present…"

2. Your family is visiting your sister on a Saturday morning, and she's just introduced you to her new neighbor, Jodi Grahn. The most welcoming response for your children would be…

   A. "It's nice to meet you, Mrs. Grahn."

   B. "Good morning!"

   C. "It's nice to make your acquaintance, Mrs. Grahn."

3. When introducing two people, you should…

   A. give their names only

   B. give their names and a bit of information about each person

   C. Give a bit of information about each person if that person is a family member. Otherwise, in respect for the person's privacy, don't share anything more than her name.*

"All the other seats are taken, so I guess it's just you and me, Philip!" I said, smiling to our church's newcomer as I waved at my husband, Kent, at the opposite end of the crowded fellowship hall. Philip and I settled in to our metal folding chairs with our plates full of the delicious foods that characterize Southern church socials. Philip's wife, Lynn, had found a seat next to Kent, and she smiled and waved back. Little did I realize that sitting at separate tables had set me up for one of the more embarrassing social blunders of my life.

Knowing that a person feels more included and welcomed when you use his name, I made sure to use Philip's often as we talked. I began by asking him, "Philip, you mentioned your family moved to Orlando last year. Where did you move from?" During our 35-minute lunch I sprinkled his name in the conversation as liberally as I sprinkle sugar in my coffee.

Philip was animated, he asked questions about the church, and he smiled often. After lunch, we rejoined Kent and Lynn and walked together back to our minivans. As we all said goodbye, I said sincerely, "It was a joy meeting you, Lynn and Philip. I hope you'll come back."

As I was buckling Corbett into his car seat, Kent asked me, "Hon, why did you call David, Philip?"

"Because that's his name," I answered matter-of-factly.

"No, his name is David. I'm positive," Kent replied, a little alarmed at my apparent mistake.

"Honey," I assured Kent, "his name can't be David. I called him Philip all through lunch, and he never said a thing about it."

As Kent pulled out of the church parking lot onto the highway, he was shaking his head. "Well, Mrs. Manners Mentor, I'm positive his name is David, so what's the etiquette for fixing this?"

"I know," I said. "I'll call Lacey. She knows their names." I dug through my purse, found my cell phone, and called her.

"Lacey, hello! It's Maralee. Your friends Lynn and her husband—they're really nice. This is a funny question, but may I ask, what is his name?"

* Answers: 1) B 2) A 3) B.*

"It's David," she answered.

My heart sank. However, on the bright side, his correct name was now forever seared in my memory.

Lynn and David returned the next Sunday. When I first saw him, the thought of changing churches crossed my mind. However, I decided apologizing was probably the sane person's choice. I caught their eyes, smiled, walked toward them and said, "Good morning, Lynn and David. David, I promise never to call you Philip again. Will you forgive me?"

They laughed a mutual sigh of relief. "Of course!" David said graciously. "I recognized your name and voice from the radio as the Manners Mentor, and I didn't know if it would be rude to correct you or not. So I just let it slide. Lynn told me on the ride home that I should have said something. I was nervous after I realized who you were. It came to me at the moment I was eating my deviled egg with my hand. I thought that both Lynn and my mom would kill me if I were eating this egg incorrectly in front of you!"

I assured him that deviled eggs are finger foods when eaten at a church picnic. We all laughed as Lynn joked that if they ever had a boy they just might name him Philip in honor of me.

Meetings Matter

Meeting new people is an adventure! Even though little embarrassments can happen, some of the best rewards in life come when we introduce two strangers and give them the opportunity to become friends.

I recently introduced a woman and a man who fell in love and were married about a year later. I've also enjoyed introducing people who were looking for the perfect job to people who were looking for the perfect employee. I'm forever thankful that a friend of mine thought, "Maralee and Kent would make a nice couple" and introduced me to my husband!

My life has been blessed a multitude of times by people who introduced me to others. Through their introductions, former strangers have become friends, business consultants, clients, household helpers, and more. Think about some of the most special people in your life, and then remember how you met. If someone introduced them to you, you owe that person a big thank-you!

Christ created us to be in relationship with Him and others. With every introduction you make, you expand people's circle of relationships. Only the Lord knows where relationships will lead, yet it's wonderful to consider that He can use us as conduits as He enriches and changes live

Because introducing two strangers is such a joy, teaching this skill to our children is also a pleasure. As with the other introduction skills, begin with the first four steps of the Five-Star First Impression (stand up, smile big, see the other person by making eye contact, and shake hands). Then use the following formula to create the perfect introduction for people who have never met.

How to Introduce Others—the Formula

As you teach these steps the first time, don't worry too much about which person should be addressed first. That skill can be added to the foundation later. (See "Growing in Graciousness" below for more details.) Just focus on learning these four simple steps.

1. *Start by saying the first person's full name.* Give both the first and last name. The names you give in the introduction should be the ones that he would use. If one or both of the other people will be referring to each other as Mr., Mrs., Pastor, Mayor, or so on, make that known in your introduction. "Pastor Hunter, I'd like to introduce Mrs. Hodson." Or "Pastor Hunter, I'd like to introduce Dr. Belton…"

2. *Then say simply, "I'd like to introduce…"* Once again, using a scripted phrase ensures that you always know the perfect thing to say. It really is a perfect phrase for introducing others. (Keep in mind that the words *to you* are implied, so you don't need to say them.) For formal, military, or governmental introductions, you can use the more formal phrase, "I'd like to present." It's best not to give commands in your introductions by saying, "Shake hands with" or "I want you to know."

3. *Say the second person's name.* Give both the first and last name in the form the person would use.

4. *Share a little bit about each person.* This little bit of information is the gift of a conversation starter. (It's nice to repeat the first names at this point, so the new acquaintances have a chance to learn the names again.)

Here's how it sounds when you put the four steps together:

Steps 1–3: "Marsha Dickinson, I'd like to introduce Bill Gentry."

Step 4: "Marsha, Bill and I met through a mutual friend who has the food blog that you enjoy reading too. He's visiting us from Texas. Bill, Marsha and I met through the radio station where I had a weekly segment. Marsha lived in Orlando. Now her job has taken her to Atlanta."

Note: Step 4 is an advanced skill for tweens and teens. Younger children can concentrate on just steps 1–3.

After that introduction, if I walk away to get everyone some iced tea, Marsha and Bill don't need to pull a conversation topic, such as the weather, out of thin air. I've given them several conversation starters: the food blog, blogging in general, Texas, Orlando, the reason for his visit, and her job transfer to Atlanta.

Out of all those topics, the most important one is their one point of connection. Can you tell what it is? If you chose the food blog, you're right. Bill and Marsha are readers of the same blog. Whenever you can think of something people have in common, you'll want to mention it because it's the quickest way to flick on the switch of friendship.

Should we expect our 11-year-olds to make this kind of detailed introduction? No, that example is at adult level. But I'll bet many children could manage this one: "Mark Thompson, I'd like to introduce Bruce Lyman. Mark and I are in the same class, and Bruce and I take karate lessons together." An 11-year-old who can make introductions like that is going to be a wonderful conduit for relationships throughout his life.

Finally, try to avoid the number one mistake of introductions. This has happened to me too many times to count. Because people are either anxious or excited to make an impression, they will start to shake hands and say, "It's nice to meet you," before the person making the introduction has finished talking. In short, don't talk over the introducer.

Growing in Graciousness
(Next-Level Skills)

Naming People in an Introduction

Whose name do you say first? The first person you name during an introduction is the person who is considered in the position of honor in that situation. Here's the short list:

- a woman before a man
- a girl before a boy
- a grown-up before a child
- a teacher before a family member, regardless of gender or age
- an elected official before a person of any gender or age
- a member of the clergy of any religion or denomination before a person of any gender or age
- a nonrelative before a relative unless introducing a child to an adult, or an adult male to an adult female

Introduce one person to a group as a whole. Don't introduce every individual in the group. One person isn't going to be able to remember a number of names at once, so it's best to introduce her to the group rather than to every individual in the group. "Everyone, I'd like to introduce Samantha Klum. Samantha is my new neighbor. She just moved here from a suburb of Chicago." Now members of the group can introduce themselves to Samantha.

Let the Adventure Begin

With just a few simple steps, you can give others the gift of a perfect introduction. If your child is five or older, now is the perfect time to begin to teach this life skill for bringing people together. It will pay dividends throughout your child's life because people appreciate those who facilitate relationships. They see them as open, caring, friendly, and eager to share. The best part is that if your children are introducing people to each other, those traits are probably true hallmarks of your children's character.

Meeting others is an adventure. Sometimes that adventure can make us regret we ever said a thing, just as

> ## *Mom to Mom*
>
> When introducing two people, share a person's name before you share his relationship to you. This puts the emphasis on the person you're introducing and not on you. For instance, if I were to introduce my husband to you, I would say, "[Your name], I'd like to introduce Kent McKee, my husband." However, most people say the relationship first: "I'd like to introduce my husband, Kent McKee." In the second introduction I've subtly made the fact that he's my husband more important than the fact that he's Kent.

when I addressed David as Philip about a dozen times in 30 minutes. Yet as I think of the people I've been able to help connect and of the people who have come into my life because someone else cared enough to introduce us, I know the adventure is worth the risk. It's one for which I want to prepare my children well so they don't miss out on a moment of it.

Inspiration and Application

1. James 2:8-9 (NIV) says, "If you really keep the royal law found in Scripture, 'Love your neighbor as yourself,' you are doing right. But if you show favoritism, you sin and are convicted by the law as lawbreakers." How is introducing people to one another a way of loving your neighbor?

2. As ambassadors for Christ, we're responsible to represent and deliver His special message to the people we come into contact with. How is introducing others an important part of the job of an ambassador? If we allow social self-consciousness to keep us from being at ease around others, how does this impact our effectiveness as ambassadors?

3. What is the four-step formula for introducing others?

4. Using the first three steps of the formula for introducing others, write the script your child would use to introduce you to Mr. Howard, the new volunteer coach.

5. Using all four steps, write a script you would use to introduce a family member to your new senior pastor. He has just moved to your city from Peru, where he has been a missionary for the past seven years.

Conversation Skills—What You Say and How You Say It

A gossip is one who talks to you about others, a bore is one who talks to you about himself, and a brilliant conversationalist is one who talks to you about yourself.

LISA KIRK

Etiquette IQ Quiz

1. During a conversation, what percentage of your message is delivered through your spoken words?

   A. 7 percent

   B. 38 percent

   C. 55 percent

2. Which of these three tips is the most important to master in order to become a gracious conversationalist?

   A. Don't interrupt the other person while he or she is speaking.

   B. Have the other person share twice as much about her life as you tell about yours.

   C. Maintain constant eye contact and good body language.

3. Your fourth grader has invited someone to come over after school to play, and the friend has said, "No thank you." When someone says "No thanks," we should teach our children to...

   A. Accept the answer and don't inquire as to why.

   B. Nicely ask why to clear the air in case something is bother-
      ing the other person.

   C. Mention the invitation again a few days later. Many people
      are too shy to say yes the first time they're asked.*

At about six months old we utter our first vowel and consonant blend:
"da-da-da-da-da." The sounds flutter from our mouths with glee and bubbles of drool, and they tickle our parents' ears with wonder and pleasure.
From that moment on we're engaged in talking—the heartbeat of relationship. Throughout life our conversations will shape our reputation, our relationships, our world.

Our first word brought joy to everyone who heard it. It powerfully
moved the hearts of the people near us. All the words we speak after that are
just as potent. Words—written, typed, texted, spoken, screamed, or whispered—affect lives. The words we speak to our children and all the words
they hear us say shape their character, their morals, and their attitude about
themselves and others. Words linger long.

THINK Before You Speak

Fabian, our family friend from Argentina, has more charisma than
almost anyone I know. His personality and positive energy turn almost
every stranger into a friend. He's always telling us about a new friend he's
excited to make our friend too. His accent stretches out his syllables, each
one electrified by his enthusiasm. When he shares with me about someone, he always begins by saying, "*Maraleeee*, you have to meet *herrr*. She's
sooo niiiiice!"

Nice!

Isn't that what we all want others to say about us and our family?
Whether they are nice is another of the first things we want to know about
the people in our lives. If we haven't met our new boss, coworker, pastor,
child's teacher, or neighbor yet, we'll look for someone who has and ask, "Is
he nice?" If the answer is yes, we breathe a sigh of relief.

We were born into sin. Therefore, self-centeredness is our preset button.
To be other-centered is a learned behavior and an act of our will. People assess

---

* Answers: 1) A 2) B 3) A.

our words and tone of voice to determine whether we are nice or unkind. Psalm 19:14 (NIV) says, "May these words of my mouth and this meditation of my heart be pleasing in your sight, LORD."

A printout of the following acronym is on my refrigerator door. It's a filter our family uses for the words we say. It reminds us to THINK before we speak and consider whether our words will build up or tear down.

> T—Is it true?
> H—Is it helpful?
> I—Is it inspiring?
> N—Is it necessary?
> K—Is it kind?

If it's not any of the above, do we really need to speak it into the person's life?

Speaking Without Words

Before we delve into the how-to of great conversation, we need to be aware of two things that we communicate to others before we say our first word—our appearance and our body language. If the words we say conflict with the message we send through nonverbal means, the nonverbal always wins.

So if your 16-year-old shows up for his first interview for a job at Burgers & Such wearing blue jeans and a T-shirt, his nonverbal message will override his verbal messages.[1] The potential employer will not take him seriously. Like it or not, our clothing announces us from across the room. It speaks for us before we've had the opportunity to say the first word.

In other words, what the eye sees, it believes. When we see someone who is attractive and nicely put together, our brain says, "This person must be popular, positive, smart, and successful." It seems unfair, but it's a fact that attractive people and those who are well dressed are received more favorably than others.

Our DNA largely determines our natural attractiveness, but we can make an effort to look our best and dress to fit the occasion. It's important to share with our children that the way we present ourselves impacts people's ability to hear what we say. That's why our children need to dress appropriately whether it's their first day of fifth grade or their first job interview. When in doubt about what to wear, it's usually better to be one step over-dressed than one step underdressed.

In addition to our appearance, what other ways do we deliver our non-verbal message? The next two big factors are our body language and our tone of voice. As moms we know something about the power of body language. We're well versed in using "the look." A head tilt combined with an unblinking gaze can tell a tween, "You're treading on thin ice." We don't have to say a word. Similarly, our children's rolled eyes, sighs, and hands on the hips shout across the room, "Mom, this isn't fair!"

Our tone of voice is amazingly powerful. We ask our teen how she's feeling, and finally she simply responds, "Fine." Yet we know immediately from her tone that she is anything but fine.

We want our tone of voice and body language to match what we're saying. When you say "Thank you" or "Please forgive me" or "I love you," say it with your whole body, or the hearer won't take it to heart.

Body Language Basics

In my Manners Mentor classes, I teach students that body language consists of three basic elements:

> the way you stand
>
> what you do with your hands
>
> your facial expressions

When our words and body language are in agreement, what we say is received and understood correctly. Here are some basics for projecting a positive, friendly message.

Stand up quickly. If you are seated and you see someone walking toward you, stand up. This shows you're literally rising to the occasion. You're eager to welcome him and honored to see him.

Stand straight. Standing up is the right thing to do, but if you stand up and then lean against something, you appear bored or tired. Evidently the other person is so draining you need to be propped up to continue being with him.

Shake hands. As he approaches, already have your hand extended to shake hands. This shows that you're not fearful or put off by him. It's the safe and polite way we physically connect with others.

Keep your hands in check. After shaking hands, let them fall naturally by your side. Putting them in your pockets (boys and men do this often) sends a subconscious message that you're not being totally open with the person or that you have something you'd like to hide (an actual item or even just a thought). In a similar way, putting your hands behind your back or folding them across your chest signals that you're closing yourself off from the other person.

Stop eating and drinking. When you're first talking with someone, put down your food or beverage. You want to welcome him with open hands and let him know he is your first priority right now. After a minute or two you can say, "Please continue! I'm going to finish my piece of cake while you tell me more about your new puppy."

Smile and make eye contact. A smile is your nonverbal signal that you're glad to have noticed someone. Maintaining eye contact shows that she has your attention. If she is talking with you, don't look away at your cell phone or let your eyes wander around the room. When you break eye contact, she senses you're no longer fully interested in her or what she's saying.

Use body language to encourage the person to continue talking. Throughout the conversation, give the other person the green light to continue. You do this by smiling, nodding your head, and mirroring her facial expressions. For example, if she is telling a story about a sad event in her life, her face will show her feelings. Your face should reflect a similar feeling.

Verbally encourage the person to continue. Don't interrupt the person while she is speaking, but it's nice to use your voice to encourage her to continue sharing. While she's speaking, say an occasional word, such as "yes," "really," "interesting," "go on," or "wow."

Resist the urge to interrupt. As much as possible, allow people to finish speaking without interrupting. When we interrupt someone, we turn everyone's attention away from him and steal his moment in the limelight. However, it's fine to interrupt briefly to ask for clarification.

The Number One Conversation Tip

With our appearance and body language in check, let's turn our attention to our words. It's easy for us and our children to become admired conversationalists if we put into practice the one trait that all great conversationalists share. (I'm referring to people who are admired for their warmth, friendliness, and caring, not to those who entertain others so they can bask in the spotlight. Those people make great party guests, but they are self-focused friends.)

The master tip—draw the other person out. People enjoy talking with those rare individuals who understand conversation is an opportunity to give to others by letting them shine.

Share only half as much about yourself as the other person does. It's counterintuitive, but it works because most people's favorite topic (even though they don't know it) is themselves. They won't find you or your life lackluster. They'll be glad to have talked with you because of your caring and interest. They will feel warmed as you let them bask in the spotlight.

I was having lunch one day with a girlfriend who is a psychologist. She shared that her new patients in the previous couple of weeks had not come to her because of major life traumas but because they didn't have anyone who would simply listen to them. They were so in need of

> ## *Mom to Mom*
>
> After you stand up to greet someone, remain standing if you'll only be speaking to her for a moment. As soon as you sense that a conversation is starting, offer her a seat. If she says, "I'd rather stand," remain standing if you can. If you get tired, after a few minutes you can nicely say, "Please continue—I'm going to sit and get comfortable," or something similar.

expressing themselves that they paid $120 for a stranger to lend them an ear for an hour.

When we happily listen to people for free, they find us priceless.

How to Teach Conversation Skills—Play Catch

The best way to encourage someone to share about himself in conversation is by asking other-centered, open-ended questions. This is an especially hard concept for children to grasp because formulating the questions entails some thought and requires children to turn the spotlight on the other person. About ten years ago while teaching a class, I came up with a game to teach the skills that work (with continued practice) every time. I call it conversation catch.

The purpose of the game is to teach children the difference between open and closed questions and to help them understand that actively participating in the conversation means more than answering questions with just a yes or no. In fact, not answering a question in a complete sentence and adding to it with a question or comment in return means they've dropped the conversation ball.

To play, all you need is one or more children and a spongy ball. First explain to your child that there are two types of questions to ask in a conversation—open and closed.

An open question can't be answered with yes or no. They're the best kind because they produce answers that share new information about the person you're talking with and propel the conversation forward. Closed questions can be answered with yes or no or a simple fact. They make conversations difficult because every time someone replies, you have to think of another question to ask. Here are a few examples of each:

Closed: "Do you like pizza?"
Open: "What are some of your favorite foods?"
Closed: "Do you have any brothers or sisters?"
Open: "Tell me about the people in your family."
Closed: "What's your favorite class?"
Open: "What do you like best about your favorite subject?"

After describing open and closed questions to your child, help him come up with an example or two. Then explain that answering someone's question with a full sentence instead of "yeah" or "yes," and adding a comment or question, shows that he's happily taking part in the conversation and not simply answering out of obligation.

Now you're ready to play!

Ask an open-ended question and then toss the ball to your child. When he catches it, he needs to answer your question in a full sentence and either add a comment or ask you an open-ended question in reply. Then he tosses the ball back to you, and you do the same. The game continues back and forth.

The first time I play the game with a student, I intentionally "drop the conversation" by not even trying to catch the ball when she tosses it back to me. As the ball falls to the ground and I pretend to be bored, she realizes what it's like to have someone hear you but not be interested in what you're saying.

Mom to Mom

Open-ended questions are the way to go, but don't go too far with them when you're first meeting someone. As adults we should change topics after we ask several questions on the same subject. If we stay on the same topic for too long, our attempt to promote pleasant conversation can feel like an interrogation to the other person.

If more than one child is playing, the ball may be tossed to anyone at any time. Throw the ball back and forth four or five times or until the conversation reaches a natural close. The first one to let the conversation drop by not adding anything to it loses. The game then starts again with a new open-ended question.

I've been able to engage the shyest of little ones and the sulkiest of teens in conversation using this method. It's great to play conversation catch a few times in the days leading up to an event where your child will be interacting with new people. By using conversation scenarios that are likely to come up at the event, you'll help your child feel more confident. After all, no one likes being at a loss for words.

Bringing Out Everyone's Best

The Ritz Carlton is known for its beautiful resorts and the legendary hospitality and care that the staff shows to each guest. One of its corporate values is that all associates are "ladies and gentlemen serving ladies and gentlemen."

I keep a similar sentiment in mind when talking to my sons: Inside each boy is a royal prince and a royal pain. The one I speak to is the one who will answer! The habit of always speaking as a lady to my two princes has been a powerful parenting tool for me. It has paid great dividends in the way they see themselves and speak to others.

Here are some conversational do's and don'ts that will help us and our children encourage the royals and discourage the pains!

Conversation Do's

Choose topics everyone can share in. If your children are talking with three friends about karate, yet only two of the others attend classes, the remaining child is left without anything to contribute. Conversations should be inclusive rather than isolating.

Summarize a conversation for a newcomer. In a sentence or two, share with the person joining a conversation what the topic is about. "Hello, Simone! We're talking about how many months each of us have until we can get our driver's permit."

Excuse yourself if you yawn. Nothing signals "I'm bored" quite like a yawn. If you yawn, apologize and explain if possible. "Excuse me, Mattie. I was up late last night." Otherwise, the speaker will wonder if he is a human sleeping pill.

Say something about what the person just said. Before changing the subject, make sure to comment on what was just said. Otherwise the person feels as if his words were disregarded. "Hearing you talk about Colorado makes me want to go there for spring vacation. Hey, have you heard anything about the new frozen yogurt place that opened up last week?"

Find the answer when you don't know it. No one is expected to be an expert on everything. When you don't know an answer, don't take a chance on giving the wrong information. But also don't say, "I don't know," and leave it at that. Doing so makes you sound disinterested and unmotivated. Instead, offer to help find the answer. "I'm not sure when the fall festival is. I think it's this Saturday. I'll check the church website and let you know."

Say when you're wrong or sorry. A weak person can't make a strong apology. If you've said something that you regret or that hurt someone's feelings or reputation, apologize. "Jess, I was wrong to yell. Please forgive me."

When someone says no, accept the decision graciously. No is a hard answer to accept, especially for children. Teach them that a no in general conversation or a no response to an invitation ("Can you come over after school today?") should be accepted without hesitation, begging, whining, or interrogation. Our tweens and teens especially need to understand that a true friend will never pressure them to do something they don't feel right in doing. When they say no to alcohol, drugs, sex, and so on, others should accept their decision without hesitation.

Speak to others in complete sentences. It's still true: "Hey" is for horses. Remember to speak to others in full sentences, even in passing: "Good morning, Joshua!" In conversation, keep the conversation ball bouncing by adding on a comment or asking a question. "It's really cold out today! Do you think it might snow?"

Speak with a cooperative spirit. Don't go into a difficult conversation looking simply to win. Respect the other person and seek mutual agreement and reconciliation. We can't control the other person's words or tone, but we can ours. Relationships will always contain the seeds of conflict. We need to model difficult discussions for our teens to show them that personal conflicts can exist and be resolved without combat.

Conversation Don'ts

Don't speak in a foreign language. Since the Tower of Babel, languages have separated us. Nothing makes someone feel more like an outsider than not being able to understand what's being said. If someone in the group doesn't speak both languages and you do, it's kind to interpret the conversation.

Don't brag, but do share about yourself and your interests. Saying that your team won the regional soccer championships is fine. Saying that the reason your team won is because you scored the final two goals is bragging.

Don't use a loud voice. Loud voices are intimidating and make people anxious and ill at ease. One of my sons had a teacher who spoke so loudly and with such a harsh tone that we had to change schools. Our son came home each day with his spirit crushed and his head full of anxiety and fear. The teacher assured my husband and me that she wasn't being cruel, but the tone she used when she said it told us the truth.

Don't say everything you're thinking. You and I know better than to say whatever pops into our heads. However, if our children, tweens, or teens see a few snippets of reality TV shows, they're going to think that in reality you can and should speak what's on your mind. (Remember the THINK acronym from earlier in the chapter.)

Don't whisper. When people near us are whispering, we need a high dose of self-confidence not to think they're talking about us even if we don't know them! When you need to speak to someone privately, say so in your regular tone and then go into another room or agree to speak at a later time. Make sure to let her know it's not bad news or an emergency. "Angela, everything is okay. I do need to speak to you privately for a minute. I'll be in the lobby after church."

Don't point out when someone misspeaks. Correcting others embarrasses them. Unless some harm will come by not correcting what was said, it's best not to bring attention to the matter. For instance,

Mom to Mom

The Bible tells us that gossiping is a sin. The temptation is so strong that if we don't pray about it, we'll fall prey to it. And psychologists warn us of an odd side effect of gossip—what we say about others, others ascribe to us. If we gossip that Caroline has a wandering eye, that Devin spends more time at work posting on Facebook than calling clients, or that Lynn lets her kids run wild, the people we tell it to will soon visualize those same traits in us. Gretchen Rubin mentions this in her wonderful book *The Happiness Project*.[2] It's called *spontaneous trait transference*. People hang the critical things we say about others on us. The good news is that the opposite is also true. When we speak well about others, people credit us with those same positive traits.

if your friend says she lives on the east side of town and you know it's the south, you don't need to mention it. If she tells everyone, "I'll see you all at practice tonight at six thirty," and you know it starts at seven, you would want to avert a mix-up. You could say, "The e-mail that was sent earlier this week said we'd be starting at seven tonight."

Don't tease. There's no such thing as innocent teasing. Jabs linger in hearts and minds, leaving the recipient to wonder if they are true.

Don't talk about what you don't like. We all have a list of likes and dislikes. When we share our dislikes—even of everyday things, such as TV shows, books, music, food, fashion, and so on—we're focusing on negatives. Talking about our likes instead is more positive for all concerned.

Questions That Are Off-Limits

Friendly, open-ended questions encourage conversation and move it forward, but some questions are embarrassing, personal, or out of place and will douse the conversation with awkwardness. Children are open and inquisitive by nature, so we need to share these off-limits topics with them privately so they're prepared for polite public conversation. Here are a few topics to keep in mind as you compose your family's list.

Are your parents divorced? Don't ask about family relationships or custody arrangements.

Why is your brother so fat? Don't ask about why someone looks the way they do.

How did you get that scar on your arm? Don't ask about accidents, sickness, or disabilities.

What neighborhood do you live in? Where someone lives may indicate their socioeconomic status. Asking where someone lives is similar to asking her about the cost of something she owns.

Ending Conversations on a High Note

We're not in the habit of hanging up the phone without saying goodbye. However, face-to-face conversations include visual cues, so some people (especially children and teens) think simply walking away is fine. In reality, the people we're sharing our conversation with deserve a pleasant ending. So how do we end our conversations on a high note? We do this by saying goodbye and opening the door (when appropriate) for the next time we'll be in contact with the person. Here are a few examples you could share with your children.

With a friend: "It's time for me to go home for dinner, Janet. I'll text you later tonight."

With a teacher: "Goodbye, Mrs. Armstrong. I'll see you tomorrow."

With an adult friend of yours: "Goodbye, Ms. Hyatt. I hope to see you again soon."

ℰ𝒱om to ℰ𝒱om

Bragging is a sign of low self-esteem in adults and children. It's a ladder of words we build when we don't feel we're high enough in the world's eyes. If you overhear your child bragging, seek ways to boost his view of himself. Share with him what you see that's great about him. Rather than praising his accomplishments (sports, art, music, grades), mention his character traits that you admire (patience, kindness, gentleness, truthfulness, and so on)—even if some of those traits aren't fully developed yet. We are all works in progress. Compliment your child when you see even the slightest hint of the trait. "Trevor, I noticed the gentle way you talked to Bella when she fell. Your comfort and kind words made her feel better. You were a very thoughtful big brother. I admire that in you." The more you acknowledge the traits you want in your child, the more those traits will start appearing.

We're Known by Our Words

Words shape lives. Through them we make ourselves known to others. Our words and actions mold the hearts, minds, values, and character of our children. When we THINK before we speak and talk to others with kindness, care, and patience (and listen in like manner), we draw out the prince or princess within our child and show him or her the path to successful relationships. This path is paved with kind, other-centered conversations that let other people know we care. This leaves them feeling glad to know us because, as my friend Fabian would say, we're "sooo niiiiice!"

Inspiration and Application

1. Colossians 4:5-6 says, "Make the most of every opportunity. Be gracious in your speech. The goal is to bring out the best in others in a conversation, not put them down, not cut them out." Were you surprised to learn that the number one tip for being a great conversationalist is to say little and be a great listener? It's freeing to remember that we don't need to impress or keep up with someone; we just need to care about getting to know him or her. How will this fact change the way you meet, greet, and talk with people? How can you encourage your child with this truth?

2. Proverbs 21:23 instructs us, "Watch your words and hold your tongue; you'll save yourself a lot of grief." Wouldn't it be great to have a time machine so we could go back and stop ourselves from saying something that caused harm in ways we couldn't anticipate at the time? Think of an incident where you would use the time machine. If your child is old enough, share the story with her and point out that your words have lingered for years. Let her see that you're not perfect but that you're growing in grace. (Some people say that the best teacher is experience, but that may not always be true. Sometimes the best teacher is someone else's experience!) Journal briefly about your story.

3. Playing conversation catch is a great way to teach about open-ended questions and conversation skills. What are the first two fun topics you'll use to play this teaching game with your children, tweens, and teens?

4. Look back over the list of conversational do's. Which three will you pass on to your child first?

5. Look back over the list of conversational don'ts. Which three will you pass on to your child first?

8

Compliments—the Seeds of Destiny

Flatter me, and I may not believe you. Criticize me, and I may not like you. Ignore me, and I may not forgive you. Encourage me, and I may not forget you.
WILLIAM ARTHUR WARD

Etiquette IQ Quiz

1. When is a compliment due a hostess?

    A. when you're a guest for a meal in her home

    B. when your hostess pays you a specific compliment

    C. when you're her guest for a meal in a restaurant

2. When should you be certain to reciprocate a compliment you were just given?

    A. every time you're given one

    B. It's never required.

    C. when you've been complimented on your appearance or something you're wearing

3. It's best to compliment your child...

    A. when she accomplishes something new

    B. on her character

    C. whenever she attempts to learn something new*

Answers: 1) A 2) B 3) B.*

A sincere compliment I received two decades ago has impacted my life in a hundred ways and counting. My marriage, ministry, and Manners Mentor career—even this book—were all born out of a solitary unexpected accolade.

The compliment came from my earth science professor during my sophomore year in college. He was dour, demanding, and unsympathetic to the feelings of his students. He was my Goliath. The stone in my slingshot was the 25-minute oral report required to pass his class.

The professor was known for making caustic remarks at the end of each student's presentation. He was more brutal than any reality-show judge. Several female students ran from the room crying, some even before he finished his critique. A few male students left cursing, their four-letter words swirling around them in a tornado of anger as they stormed down the hall.

The professor had the students present in alphabetical order. My maiden name is Thompson, so I was one of the last to speak. I had worked hard all semester on my report. Still, having watched almost 65 of my classmates suffer his verbal assaults, I was trembling as I walked to the front of the class to give my presentation on soil erosion. When I finished, in anticipation of his remarks, I grasped the sides of the lectern to brace myself and to help hide my shaking hands.

The professor was silent, contemplating. That was a first. His crushing attacks had always come quickly. Then he stood up. He had never done that before either. As he stood, his metal folding chair scraped the linoleum floor like fingernails on a chalkboard. The class cringed.

I knew immediately that my presentation had affected the professor differently from the others. I feared this was going to be his harshest review. I panicked.

"Mar-a-lee? Is that how you pronounce your name?"

"Yes, sir," I answered with politeness and hesitation.

"Class!" he barked out. "Look at Maralee and listen to me."

He continued, "She's done something that has never been done in my almost ten years of listening to mediocre, to put it nicely, presentations. Miss Thompson…"

The room spun around me. The night before I had promised myself I wouldn't cry, but now I didn't care as I felt tears threaten to break through my dam of determination. I inhaled hard, trying not to faint.

Without any tenderness of tone he continued, "You have given the first great presentation I've ever heard. I'm giving you an A-plus for the semester. You are a communicator. I suggest you don't let that talent go to waste."

The room stopped revolving. I exhaled. "Thank you, sir," was all I could think to say. As I took my seat, the class erupted in applause.

Spiritual CPR

Proverbs 18:21 (AMP) tells us, "Death and life are in the power of the tongue, and they who indulge in it shall eat the fruit of it [for death or life]."

Over and over again, my professor's words have served as mental and spiritual CPR, breathing life into my hopes and blowing away my doubts. Seven years later God used that compliment to overpower my cowardice and give me the courage to step onstage on the one-year anniversary of my first husband's death to share my testimony…our story…God's work.

It was the start of my ministry.

That evening the woman who would introduce me to Kent just 12 weeks later was in the audience. As I spoke from the lectern, God spoke to her heart: "Introduce Kent to Maralee."

Four years after that evening, the echo of the professor's compliment gave me the courage to accept my first speaking engagement on business etiquette. It was the start of my etiquette career.

My classes, presentations, and seminars gave me the confidence to talk to the first reporter who called me. That gave me the confidence to go on the radio for the first time, which led to TV, which led to my blog, which led to this book.

One compliment changed my life, and it continues to do so. Now that compliment is benefiting my children. I'm a more confident, positive, encouraging mom and a better example to my children because of the experiences that compliment prompted.

The Gift That Can't Be Lost, Broken, or Stolen

Within us is the power to change people's lives, alter their destinies, and impact generations. And it's so easy. We don't even need to know the other people well. When you give someone a compliment, you give a gift that is stored where it can never be lost, broken, or stolen. It's stored in the person's heart. Every heartbeat circulates esteem, confidence, and possibilities throughout the recipient.

Not every compliment changes a life, but our kind words often create a butterfly effect beyond what we will ever know. Proverbs 25:11 (NIV) says, "Like apples of gold in settings of silver is a ruling rightly given." A compliment is as beautiful and valuable as any piece of fine jewelry from Tiffany's—something to be treasured, admired, and remembered.

Even if our words only manage to bring a momentary smile to a frazzled mom or give a child with a daunting task the confidence to try, isn't that reason enough to share them?

When we compliment others, we model for our children the language of praise. When our compliments are directed toward our children, we meet their profound need for verbal proof of our love. We also give them examples (and there are so many!) of how special they are to Christ and to us. "Luke, I admire the way you're gentle with your little brother when you play. This afternoon I noticed how you kept running to get the ball for him every time you threw it and he missed. You didn't get frustrated. Just like Jesus, you're a patient and kind teacher!"

The Bible tells us that God inhabits (He lives within) the praises of His people. I love the picture I have in my mind of Him basking in the sweet faint sounds of praises rising from earth to His throne room in heaven. Just think—our praises are the soundtrack of heaven. Because we are made in His image, we and our children naturally thrive in a space where compliments and praises are plentiful.

Complimenting our children, family, friends, and even strangers on something they've done is wonderful, but we also need to recognize that there are other types of compliments. The best compliments aren't for what people have done (what they've written, drawn, built, sung, danced, scored, accomplished, or earned). The praise that keeps people growing in character is praise for their character. When a loved one is frustrated, sad, angry, resentful, ill, or losing hope, a reminder of her best qualities can lift her thoughts and actions out of the fog of funk and back into the light of truth.

Compliments Are More than Ego Boosters

A compliment is a gift from your heart, so it's as unique as you are. No one else can give exactly the same gift. That's why it's important for each of us to compliment others as often as we have the opportunity. We're the only ones who can deliver that exact message to the person.

Often people have a hard time seeing their own abilities or best traits. When we compliment them, we spotlight a quality they might not otherwise know they have.

Unfortunately, we live in a tear-down culture. Traits like purity, self-restraint, and delayed gratification are seen as disposable today. When you compliment good character, the recipient feels appreciation for a character trait that she might not have felt before. She is then more likely to value that character trait herself.

A mom might say to her high school daughter, "Vanessa, I see the way the guys look at you when you walk by. I know lots of them ask you out. I admire the way you're concentrating on school and waiting on God to bring you a boyfriend handpicked for you."

As we seek the good in others, we grow in grace. Our compliments benefit both us and the other people, and our compliments reaffirm the value of kindness in general.

Compliments Versus Flattery

It's said that for every godly trait, Satan has a perversion of it. For instance, to be a faithful friend is godly. To allow yourself to be walked on, to have your feelings disregarded, or to give and never receive is a perversion. That relationship would better be described as a master-servant contract rather than a friendship.

There is a perversion of compliments as well—flattery. Compliments are powerful tools for equipping others. Yet Satan, given the chance, will make us feel flattery is necessary in order to fully compliment the person.

Let me share with you the difference between flattery and compliments. Compliments are always the truth. They express your sincere respect, appreciation, affection, or admiration. Flattery might or might not be based on truth. However, flattery is motivated by self-interest. Satan distorts the Christlike trait of seeking out and responding to the kindness of others into a type of hero worship. The flatterer puffs someone up so he can win favor and get people to like him. Flattery is also used to assure someone everything is all right when the truth is not positive.

> ## *Mom to Mom*
>
> Some adults are slow to compliment other adults lest they inflate the other person's ego and downplay their own strengths. Don't worry. People won't think less of you when you compliment them. After all, you must be insightful and smart—look who you're savvy and wise enough to compliment!

If you find yourself or your child flattering someone, examine why this person's acceptance is so important to you. What need do you want this person to meet? Bring that empty spot before the Lord and allow Him to fill it. A friendship begun by flattery will never be equal. You'll always be left carrying the bags and walking two paces behind the other person.

Giving a Compliment People Will Always Remember

Are you ready to start blessing those around you with compliments? Follow these three guidelines to make the most of every compliment.

Say the person's name. As you learned from the Five-Star First Impression, say the person's name if you know it. The compliment will resonate more when it includes her name, the verbal marker tied most to her identity.

Speak in a complete sentence. An enthusiastically spoken "Nice!" is, well...nice, but it isn't exactly a compliment you can hang your future on.

Be very specific. When you're complimenting someone you know, put forethought into your words and say the compliment at your first opportunity.

"Nice jump ball in the third quarter, Anderson! You've been practicing hard, and your defense skills are amazing to watch!"

Some Great Compliment Starters

Are you tongue-tied when you want to motivate and encourage someone with a compliment? Here are ten super ways to start:

1. "I admire the way you…"
2. "I noticed how you…."
3. "You have a great skill for…"
4. "You amaze me at how you…"
5. "I appreciate the way you…"
6. "You make our family better because of the way you…"
7. "You did a great job with…"
8. "You brought up such good ideas. I especially liked…"
9. "You bring joy into the room when you…"
10. "You set an example for everyone to follow by the way you…"

When Compliments Are Required

Compliments are a type of gift, and like other gifts (wedding, baby shower, birthday party, Christmas), sometimes one is required. Compliments should be given to recognize special milestones, effort, achievements, and such. Our children need to know when compliments are in order so they're not out of step socially and so they (and we) don't miss an opportunity to give the gift of noticing. Here are times when compliments are especially nice.

Snacks or meals. During or after a meal, a compliment is due the home chef. If you're being treated to a meal in a restaurant, compliment the host on his great choice of restaurants. After your first few bites, if complimenting the food seems like stretching the truth, substitute a sincere thank-you for the invitation to dinner rather than commenting on the food.

Awards. When someone you know wins an award or receives special recognition, take the opportunity to compliment her on her achievement. It doesn't matter whether she is Student of the Week or *Time* magazine's Person of the Year.

Weddings. You'll want to compliment the bride on how beautiful she looks (*all* brides are beautiful), and compliment the groom on his great taste in women. It's also kind to tell the couple what you enjoyed about the ceremony and reception.

Speeches and presentations. Whether your daughter's friend just sang at the school's annual parent night, your sister taught this week's Bible study, or your neighbor appeared as a guest on *Good Morning, America*, when you meet someone who has recently spoken publicly, it's nice to compliment her. If you can congratulate her on a job well done, that's great. If not, then compliment her on her bravery in speaking in front of others. After all, the two biggest fears most people have are falling and public speaking.

Someone shows you something he created. If someone shows you something he created, a compliment is in order. (This applies to a person of any age!) If you don't feel you can honestly compliment the quality of the end product, compliment the idea and the effort.

"Thank You Very Much!"

I adore birds. Look in every room of my home, and you'll find one or more decorative elements featuring our fine-feathered friends. Let's say you share my fondness for birds. In fact, you and I have bird pictures hanging on our walls, bird plates in our kitchen cabinets, bird pillows on our sofa, and bird ornaments decking our Christmas tree every year.

For your birthday, I search for hours online at Etsy to find you a delicate, handcrafted bluebird necklace. I find one from an up-and-coming jewelry artist in the Midwest. I like it so much that I would buy myself one, but… well, I can't afford two. And besides, I want this gift to be yours alone. I wrap it with care, picking out the perfect paper and tying the bow just so.

Your birthday arrives, and while we're at lunch I excitedly hand you the gift. You unwrap it with abandon, but when you open the lid of the jewelry box, your smile disappears as you wrinkle your forehead and say, "Really? The bird is kind of small. I prefer bolder jewelry."

That reaction would never happen in real life, would it? Who would be that ungrateful? That insensitive? That rude? No, a person doesn't usually react that way when the gift comes wrapped with a bow. However, when the gift is a compliment, people react that way a lot—a whole lot. If we knew we were doing it, we'd be aghast. It's just that we don't realize our actions.

It happens because we've been taught not to brag about ourselves. We must stay humble and cautious of vanity. We were taught correctly not to boast about ourselves. But our teachers forgot to tell us that we are not supposed to shoot down compliments other people direct toward us. A compliment is a gift from another person's heart, and when we try to downplay it, deny it, or disagree with it, we throw the gift back in her face.

Several years ago an acquaintance of mine cut her long hair into a chin-length bob. I ran into her at Starbucks a few days after she had it done. "Linda, your haircut is stylish! You look beautiful, as always," I said happily.

"Maralee, you're kidding me. I hate this haircut. It's hideous. How could you like it?"

I felt awful. "Linda," I said, "I would never purposefully hurt you or flatter you. My compliment was sincere. But since you don't like your hairstyle, I hope it grows out quickly for you." I picked up my feelings and my tall mocha latte and left.

As with any gift, a compliment should be accepted graciously and the giver thanked—regardless of whether we agree with the compliment. Here's how.

Reply to the compliment in a complete sentence. Saying "thank you" doesn't necessarily show the giver that we appreciate the compliment. We can do better by using complete sentences, including her name (if we know it), and mentioning what she complimented us for. Your ten-year-old might say to her friend, "Tia, it was nice of you to say you liked my drawing. Thank you!"

Don't disagree with the compliment. This is like telling someone he has bad taste.

Don't add self-deprecating remarks. There's no need to downplay someone's compliment. When you do, you're putting qualifiers on her statement.

Don't expand on the compliment. There's no need to give the verbal equivalent of a touchdown victory dance. "I was better than good today. I played my best game ever!"

A thank-you is always in order. Even if you don't agree with the compliment, the correct response is a simple thank-you sentence.

Special Tips for Complimenting Your Children

Corbett, my youngest, has a fascination with costumes, especially masks. He'll make seven or more paper masks in a day. Superheroes, knights, wrestlers, clowns...he finds all of them fascinating to design, draw, cut out, and color. I follow the trail of paper scraps, scattered crayons, and markers through the house until I find him sitting on the floor, a pile of his paper creations surrounding him. He's eager to show and explain each one to me in minute detail! "Let's start with this one, Mommy. I'll tell you how I thought of it. I was...."

> ### *Mom to Mom*
>
> There's no need to reciprocate compliments. If you were planning on sharing one, don't keep it to yourself. However, if you weren't, that's fine. Reciprocating compliments often seems as if you're trying to think of something nice to say simply to be on equal ground with the other person. It lessens his remark. Allow him the gift of gifting you!

Some of them amaze me. I am awed that he envisioned the mask in his mind and then made it out of paper and tape. Other masks he makes? Well, they look like what they are—two-minute creations made by a little boy who scribbled colors on paper.

What to do? Compliment all of them to encourage what is obviously a delight for him and a rare talent? Or play critic and develop his taste for quality work? If I praise him too much, is he going to become vain or grow up to be a praise junkie? If I don't praise him enough, is he going to become a perfectionist? Will he never be satisfied with his work, always looking down on it because I never looked up to it?

The answer to all these questions is yes!

How do we strike a balance so we raise children who are confident in their abilities but not vain about them? Children who appreciate our praises but aren't junkies for them? Who know when the work they've done is something they can be proud of, not something they need to fix just once more? As moms, we need to know when to compliment our children and when just a comment would better serve them. Here's help in deciding which is most appropriate at the moment.

No praise junkies here. Acknowledge progress and ask your child how it makes him feel. This will help him want to succeed for personal gratification and not simply for your approval (or the approval of others). "Zak, you've been studying spelling each night instead of waiting until the night before the test. I notice it's really paying off in your grades. You've gone from a *D* to a high *C*. How does that make you feel?"

Keep vanity at bay. Praise and compliment the character behind the success instead of the success alone. "Caroline, you've been faithful in practicing your dance routines every afternoon and helping the younger girls learn their routines. You're caring and hardworking. I can see why Mrs. Armstrong picked you as the cheer team captain." Compare that type of praise to this: "Caroline, you're an amazing dancer. You nail all the routines, and you're beautiful when you do it. No wonder you're team captain this year."

Perfectionists never believe they reach their goals. I'm a recovering perfectionist. I know what it's like to do my best and yet feel that my best is not good enough. Sometimes perfectionists grow up under the wings of parents who compare their children's work to others. Or to spare their children from what they believe to be false hope, they'll be brutally honest. "You're story isn't that good, honey. To be honest, I don't think you have a talent for writing." You can comment on and encourage the action without having to falsely compliment it. The parent could have said, "You like writing, don't you! Did you like this story? I can tell! It's great to do something you enjoy. Keep doing it. I'm happy for you and proud that you put your ideas on paper."

A parent's approval is vital to the healthy self-esteem of a child. The child will keep working and working to get that approval, even after he realizes he'll never be able to reach the mark. If the parent's approval comes later (or the world applauds him), he won't feel as if the approval is warranted. He'll simply reason it away: "I was lucky with this current success because there's no way my abilities are worthy of this achievement."

Don't compliment everything. If you do, you'll have a child whose self-esteem depends on praise. As a teen and adult, if others don't adore everything she does, she'll blame people for not appreciating the wonder she is.

Don't hold back your compliments and praise. In all relationships, hard truths sometimes need to be told. That's biblical. Those situations should be dealt with quickly and with love, forgiveness, and the expectation that the action in question will change. However, that's the exception. At the center of every healthy parent–child relationship is mutual respect and admiration. Go ahead and shout from the rooftops how much you adore your children. If your children are little, they'll giggle and hug you. If they're tweens, they'll be mortified. If they're teens, they might try to change their last name. Regardless, as they mature, they'll rise up and call you blessed for freely giving them your approval.

Life Itself—Glorious Life

"Whoever goes hunting for what is right and kind finds life itself—glorious life!" (Proverbs 21:21). A dour professor I had in college gave me one compliment and changed my life. I don't know his name. I don't remember what he looked like. He scared me, yet I'm so very thankful for that man. He made one observation about a skill I didn't believe I had, and here I sit today. What about you and me? Whose life can we change? What can we inspire in our children? How can we notice what is kind and good in another and put him or her on the road to life itself—glorious life?

Inspiration and Application

1. In the brief four chapters that make up the book of Colossians, Paul sprinkled compliments throughout as he mentioned members of the church there. In Colossians 1:2, he greeted them by calling them "stalwart followers of Christ." In verses 3-5 he wrote, "Our prayers for you are always spilling over into thanksgivings. We can't quit thanking God our Father and Jesus our Messiah for you! We keep getting reports on your steady faith in Christ, our Jesus, and the love you continuously extend to all Christians. The lines of purpose in your lives never grow slack, tightly tied as they are to your future in heaven, kept taut by hope." Notice how specific Paul's compliments are. He didn't just say, "Good job, guys!" He detailed why he was so proud of the Colossians. List three specific things Paul complimented them on in these verses.

2. In Colossians 2:6, Paul gave the church guidance. "My counsel for you is simple and straightforward: Just go ahead with what you've been given. You received Christ Jesus, the Master; now live him." How can you live out Christ by complimenting others?

3. What three characteristics of compliments will you share with your children to help them understand the power of their words?

4. The life of a Christian is marked by gratitude. We can't love Christ without first being grateful for His sacrifices for us. To compliment is to express gratitude and esteem to others. Model this for your children by complimenting each of them as soon as you next see them. Write down one aspect of each of your children's character that you will compliment. Be specific and share both how you admire the trait and how you think God might choose to use it for the sake of the kingdom.

5. This week, compliment two strangers on a job well done. It can be anyone—a receptionist in your doctor's office, a grocery store cashier, or a server in a restaurant. Take note of the positive effect of your words. How did the person's facial expression change? How did it affect her mood? Did she greet the next customer with renewed vigor? How did it make you feel? Try to have your children with you. If not, make sure to tell them about it over dinner one evening. Write in a journal about your encounters.

9

Wonder Words and the Wonders They Work

God gave you a gift of 86,400 seconds today.
Have you used one to say thank you?
WILLIAM ARTHUR WARD

Etiquette IQ Quiz

1. Which of the following best defines "thank you"?

   A. I like what you did for me.

   B. I recognize that you did something for me.

   C. I appreciate you for doing what you did for me.

2. When you say, "I'm sorry," what does your apology imply?

   A. What you said or did made the other person feel bad.

   B. You promise not to do the same thing again.

   C. You did not live up to your own standards.

3. A demanding child is usually the result of...

   A. parents who give in to the demands of the child too easily

   B. parents who place too many demands on the child, causing him or her to feel overwhelmed

   C. the child's personality type*

Answers: 1) B 2) A,B,C 3) A.*

One Christmas season, I tried an experiment to see whether Wonder Words really could work wonders. I visited several businesses during the happiest time of the year, but the customers appeared to be anything but happy. More often than not, when cashiers greeted them kindly, the customers were either talking on their cell phones and ignoring the cashiers completely, or they replied with a sterile "Hey" or a dismissive "Make sure all my sale prices ring up."

My experiment started by having a brief conversation with a cashier. When the next customer approached, I ended my conversation with the cashier by saying something like this, making sure it would be overheard: "You've been so kind! I appreciate you and your Christmas spirit. Thank you for making my shopping so pleasant! I hope everyone is as kind to you as you've been to me. Thank you again, and Merry Christmas!"

Every time I did this, regardless of how tuned-out the next customer had been, he immediately smiled and began a conversation with the cashier. Even the people on their cell phones at least acknowledged the clerk. Two cell-phone users ended their conversation: "I'll call you back. I'm at the register now."

The magic of two of the Wonder Words ("thank you") completely changed the next customer's expectations and demeanor. He or she became eager to experience a similar positive interaction.

I continued my experiment all Christmas season, and it is now a habit I use daily. I find it fascinating that it has worked almost every time! If I thank the cashier, the next person in line catches a new point of view. Attitudes, moods, and expectations really are contagious, and the Wonder Words that express positive ones really do work wonders.

What Makes Them Wonder Words?

The Wonder Words are simply the six most common polite words and phrases we use in social interactions:

Please.

Thank you.

You're welcome.

Excuse me.

I'm sorry.

May I?

I call them Wonder Words because of the wonders they can speak into others' lives. In fact, the connection between etiquette and Scripture is especially clear in our choice of words. A good example is Proverbs 26, which describes the difference between controlled and caring speech versus conniving and careless words.

Controlled. Those with this speech pattern think before speaking, know when silence is best, and give wise advice.

Caring. Those with this speech pattern speak truthfully and try to encourage.

Conniving. Those with this speech pattern are filled with wrong motives, gossip, slander, and a desire to twist truth.

Careless. Those with this speech pattern are filled with lies, curses, and quick-tempered words, which can lead to rebellion and destruction.[1]

With the words we choose, we can weave either magic or mayhem in someone's life. Teaching our children to use Wonder Words makes their speech controlled and caring instead of conniving or careless.

Creating a Haven of Peace at Home

As part of my experiment, I set positive expectations for both clerks and customers, which softened their hearts and almost always led to positive interactions. As moms, we soften our children's hearts by establishing that kind, civil, and respectful words are hallmarks of our families. This is the first step in teaching our children to act and interact well. It is the cornerstone of all manners.

Imagine a home where "Give me…" "Get away," and "Whatever" are replaced with "If you have a moment, please…" "May I have…" and "Thank you for…"

It can happen!

When these words are a part of your household, you have a child who is admired by others. You have a home that is a haven of peace—a place of rejuvenation and encouragement. And you have a family who understands that Wonder Words aren't just social niceties; they're the way we esteem, acknowledge, and encourage one another. As such, they are keys to emotional health and living out Christlikeness.

So how do we teach Wonder Words?

They're not hard to teach; they just take a long time to become automatic. But a time will come when they infiltrate our children's hearts and become automatic and sincere. (Later in the chapter I'll share tips for helping your children make a habit of using Wonder Words.)

The challenge for us moms, actually, is that Wonder Words must come naturally to us if they are ever to become second nature to our children. We teach the use of these words by modeling, and we have to do a lot of modeling for these words to take hold. In fact, it's impossible to overuse them. Children will use Wonder Words only about 25 percent as often as they hear them. If you want their use to be common, you have a lot of pleasing and thanking to say yourself! However, the good news is that once using these words becomes a habit for your family, it's a hard habit to break.

We prepare our children's hearts for making these words second nature by starting at birth (yes, I mean birth!) and continuing throughout all the stages of growing up. Let's look at those steps.

Courtesy Never Grows out of Style

The vocabulary of courtesy is the first manner you teach, and you can start from birth. "Thank you for letting me change your diaper, Josiah!" Or, "May Mommy please read you this story, Mariah?"

Why start so young when babies can't even understand what we're saying? We want to make polite words plentiful so that as our children begin to copy our words, Wonder Words will be among the first they say.

In the beginning the words are simply rote. A two-year-old isn't going to understand the meaning of "please" or "thank you." That's okay because your first goal is to make a habit of saying those words. Little children don't understand why they need to take "yucky" medicine, eat vegetables, get their hair washed, and do a myriad of other things they have to do. Later they'll understand the benefit of all these things, including using their Wonder Words.

When your child is old enough (about age three), begin to explain the meaning of each Wonder Word and how using it shows our respect and appreciation for others and impacts the way people feel about themselves and us. When your child begins to say them not only from habit but also because he desires to express them, he understands the heart of manners. What once was rote is now sincere. You've done great, Mom!

These are words you never outgrow. Because the words are taught at such a young age, tweens and teens will sometimes wrongly believe they've outgrown their usage. They won't hear them often in conversations at school or on their favorite TV shows, and that seems to support their opinion. But you can remind them that people especially appreciate polite language from tweens and teens because it is so rare!

In the Manners Mentor classes I teach to this age group, I take them through a little exercise. I begin by asking them what the correct answer to five plus one was when they were in first grade. They all easily answer, six. Then I ask them what the correct answer was in fourth grade and then eighth grade. I continue by asking them what the answer will be when they're in college, when they have their first child, and when they have their first grandbaby. Each time they answer six in unison as they try to figure out what I'm getting at.

I then explain that when something is correct, it doesn't change as we get older. Saying "please" and "thank you" was polite and respectful when they were six years old just as it is today, and it still will be when they're eighty-five. Their eyes light up as they comprehend the simple fact that right is right.

Wonder Words Show Who We Are

Wonder Words are not for getting what we want but for showing who we are. It's easy for children to fall into the trap of using Wonder Words when they're hoping to gain something, such as a later bedtime, a ride to the mall, or an outing to the movies. However, using Wonder Words for personal gain alone is insincere. For manners to be more than window dressing, our children must understand that they cannot use Wonder Words like a magic wand to get their way. Instead, the words are gifts we give others and ourselves. They're for putting people around us at ease and showing the respect we have for them and ourselves. We are naturally self-centered, but these words help us to be other-centered.

Ways the Words Work Best

Wonder Words work best when used with other words. A tossed-out "thanks" or a whining "please" don't do Wonder Words justice. Here are four ways to make an expression of courtesy the highlight of someone's day:

- Smile and make eye contact with the other person.

- Speak in a complete sentence.

- Describe what you're thanking her for, asking her for, or apologizing for.

- If you know her name, include it in your sentence.

Here are some examples.

- "Thank you for the ride home from karate practice, Mrs. Poulalion!"

- "Liza, may I please borrow your blue marker to color the eyes of the person I'm drawing?"

- "You're welcome, Jackson! It was fun having you at my birthday party. Thank you for coming!"

- "Mr. West, I'm sorry for not stopping by to help you mow the lawn at ten as I said I would. Please forgive me. I know I'm late, but I'm available now if you'd still like me to help."

The Wonders of the Word World

Do you know what really convinced me that polite language was more than just a social nicety? I started explaining to my children and my Manners Mentor classes what each of these words meant. Then I realized how much these words say about our relationships. These words are about much more than being polite—they reveal what we think about those around us. You can use the following explanations to teach these deeper meanings to your own children.

Please. No one likes being taken for granted. For that reason, *please* is near the top of the list of Wonder Words. It expresses an understanding that you're asking the other person to do something for you and that you don't take her possible action for granted. Whether your child is asking her sister to pass the salt and pepper or asking you to drive across town for a playdate, she should realize she's making a request, not a demand.

The word *please* acknowledges someone's effort on your behalf and serves us well throughout life because being noticed and acknowledged meets one of our deepest emotional needs. Saying the word *please* was the first manner many of us moms taught our children. When both Marc and Corbett were starting to drink from sippy cups, I would say, "Would you like some juice?" They'd nod their tousled heads and say, "Yes!"

I'd smile and add, "Yes, what?"

They'd think for a moment, and then their eyes would light with remembrance and they'd happily say, "Please!" which both of them pronounced "Peas!" As I poured the juice, I would say, "Thank you for saying please and asking so nicely. It's my pleasure to pour you this juice!"

Thank you. These words express gratitude, which represents the wellspring of the Christian's life—our gratitude for Christ and His love, sacrifice, and forgiveness. Each time we sincerely say "thank you," our heart toward others—our testimony—grows. As you're saying the words, you momentarily stop wanting anything more. It's a pure form of contentment.

You personally recognize, publicly pronounce, and emotionally ponder the gift of kindness you just received. If you're on the receiving end, a thank-you confirms that you're valued. If you're on the giving end, it confirms that Christ's graciousness in you is pouring out to others.

You're welcome. These are probably the most overlooked Wonder Words. They are valuable for acknowledging and encouraging kindness. When you say them, you let the other person know that you heard his thank-you. It shows that you're happy to have done a nice thing for him, and that you're thankful for his thoughtfulness. It completes the circle of gratitude. To help young children remember to say "you're welcome," teach them that the two phrases go together like best friends. They don't want to be apart. Every time someone says "thank you," be sure to say "you're welcome" in reply.

Excuse me. When people are concerned about the comfort of others, they often say "excuse me." You can use the phrase whenever you say or do something that interferes, even momentarily, with another person's physical or social comfort. It's what to say when your actions are in no way intentional but you realize you've caused the other person discomfort.

You can say "excuse me" when you accidentally step in front of people, bump into them, drop or spill something on or near them, talk over them, make a sudden or loud noise, sneeze, cough, mistake them for someone else, or a million other things. It shows you realize that your words or actions were an inconvenience to them.

I'm sorry. These two words are appropriate when your actions were hurtful and not necessarily accidental. Maybe you couldn't imagine all of the consequences of your actions at the time you said or did what you did. Regardless, "I'm sorry" means that you take ownership of your hurtful words or actions and are ready to right the wrong. Saying "I'm sorry" and naming what you did wrong can clear away hurt, anger, and disappointment, and bless the other person with peace and closure.

If words have become harsh, regardless of whose fault it was, it's always good to be the first to apologize. Saying "I'm sorry" doesn't make you a doormat, and it doesn't mean you're saying the fault is all yours. Despite who began the argument, you can and should apologize for taking part in it at all. Conflict is going to occur in every relationship. However, we can step back and prevent the conflict from turning into a war of words and wills. It really does take the bigger person to apologize. By doing so you're opening the door to reconciliation and healing. I tell my boys that it's not who wins the battle that counts. The true victory goes to the one who restores peace.

Inherent in all sincere apologies is the promise that you will try not to do the same thing again, that you realize you've hurt the other person and that you didn't live up to your own standards. Otherwise, you aren't truly sorry. You're simply asking the other person to be long-suffering with your wrongdoing.

May I? These Wonder Words are also often forgotten. When you start a request with "May I?" you show that you will respect the answer whether it is yes or no. For example, "Mom, may I go with Tamara's family to a movie Saturday afternoon?" It also shows that you don't assume you know the agendas of others, and you don't plan on taking action without considering them. When a child asks, "May I please be excused from the table?" the parent will probably say yes, but he has the option to reply, "Not yet, dear." Training our children to ask to be excused from the dining table is a great way to help them to be conscious of others instead of doing whatever they want. Like all manners, this promotes a mind-set that will serve them throughout life.

As adults, we don't want to make assumptions. For example, at the end of a business meeting we might ask our supervisor, "May I go back to working on the Thompson account now?" Again, the answer is probably yes. However, either children or adults might not be aware of other plans. Mom might say, "Hold on for just a minute, Layla, Dad and I are going to tell you about the plans for this weekend." At work, the supervisor might say, "Sandra, let's hold off on working on the account until Thursday after the audit from the home office. Until then, we'll focus on getting everything in order for the compliance department."

Making a Habit of Using Wonder Words in Your Home

Victoria was visiting Sharon, her former maid of honor, at home. Sharon's seven-year-old daughter, Laura Beth, came into the family room with her juice cup empty. She handed it to her mom and said in a matter-of-fact tone, "Juice." Automatically, Sharon poured the juice, smiled, said, "Here you go, sweetie," and handed it back to her daughter. Without a word or smile, Laura Beth took the cup and headed back to her room.

Victoria was stunned at Laura Beth's demanding attitude and the fact that Sharon didn't even seem to notice that she was being ordered about by a young general who didn't even have the respect to nod in appreciation.

A few weeks later Victoria visited her friend again, but this time she was there to babysit Laura Beth. While Laura Beth colored in her room, Victoria curled up in a chair to read a book. After a few minutes, the little girl emerged from her room and said politely, "Miss Victoria, excuse me. May I please have some juice?"

"Sure, Laura Beth!" Victoria responded with enthusiasm. Filling the cup, she handed it to Laura Beth, who smiled and said, "Thank you for the juice, Miss Victoria!"

"You're very welcome, sweetie," Victoria replied. And with that Laura Beth gingerly skipped back into her room to finish the picture she was coloring as a surprise for Miss Victoria.

Why did Laura Beth approach her mom and Victoria with such different levels of kindness and respect?

The answer is *training*.

Sharon had made it clear how Laura Beth was to interact with visitors. *Please* and *thank you* were required. At home, Sharon had grown lax. She appreciated and even modeled the use of Wonder Words, but she didn't require it. So Laura Beth saved her best self for others. Mom, Dad, and her siblings were exposed to her real self.

Our goal is for our best selves to become our real selves. Here's how to make a habit of using Wonder Words so that our children use them every day!

Teach nicely. When teaching children to use Wonder Words, we need to set the example by reminding or correcting them calmly and sweetly so we don't send mixed messages. I've overheard several moms issue harsh warnings to their children: "You had better say 'thank you.' I'm tired of you taking me and everything you get for granted." Yikes! When we're stressed or worn thin, it's okay to tell our children how we're feeling, but not like that! Instead, let them know that they could really help by doing such and such right now. It shows them that even when they're frazzled they can and should keep their cool and respond in a civil manner, just like Mom!

Teach from birth. Wonder Words need to be ingrained deeply, so the earlier you start, the better.

Teach by example. Let Wonder Words flood your vocabulary. Take every opportunity to gift others with kind words.

Teach through praise. Our children and teens crave our attention and praise. Thank them for saying "thank you" and praise them for saying "please." They will give you more of whatever gets your attention, so pay lots of attention when you hear them speaking nicely.

Teach by waiting. If Wonder Words aren't forthcoming, wait for them. Don't pour the juice. Don't make the peanut butter sandwich. Don't answer when they ask if they can borrow the car. If they don't catch on, then say, "I'm waiting on you to ask me differently." For younger children you might say, "What Wonder Word could you add to what you just said?"

Teach by reminding. Children and teens need a lot of reminders if they are to make a habit of using Wonder Words. When possible, remind in advance, "Justin, when the server comes over to refill your drink, make sure to look at him, smile, and say, 'Thank you for pouring me

Mom to Mom

Do you have a demanding child or teen? One who just won't let an issue rest? Usually that's a sign that her demands are met if she keeps on demanding. You've got to break the cycle by keeping your calm and standing your ground. "Marisa, I always want to hear what you have to say. I've heard you on this matter and considered it. My answer is no, and it always will be. I understand you're disappointed and even angry because that's not the answer you wanted. I feel bad for you. However, please don't bring it up again. I'm going to work on the laundry now. Please excuse me."

The next time she tries to bring it up, say, "I'm sorry, Marisa. That subject is closed." If she begins to whine, excuse yourself and walk away. If you give in, you can expect that in the future she'll reach even higher levels of demanding behavior. As Jesus said in Matthew 5:37 (NIV), "All you need to say is simply 'Yes' or 'No'; anything beyond this comes from the evil one."

more water.' We want him to know we appreciate his efforts on our behalf and that we don't take him for granted." In this way your child or teen is prepared in advance to use Wonder Words, and when the server leaves, you get the opportunity to praise your child for expressing his appreciation.

Teach through consistency. We don't want our children to act one way at home and another out in the world. Make the use of Wonder Words non-negotiable for every member of your family. Teach nicely, of course, but don't give up until your family is characterized by their use.

Teach by role-playing. Prior to an event, think of possible opportunities your child will have to use Wonder Words and role-play ways she can use them in conversation. Teach by pointing out others' behavior. When children on TV sitcoms are insensitive or demanding, they receive applause. Children and teens can think this makes rudeness okay for the real world. Watch TV together and point out missed opportunities for using Wonder Words and how the response of the other characters might have been different if they had talked to one another in a respectful manner.

Thank You for Reading This Chapter

Wonder Words really are the wonders of the word world. They develop caring and controlled tongues in our children and us. They express our respect, regard, and gratitude for others. When we use them consistently, they become beautiful hallmarks of our character. As my Christmas experiment taught me, our kind words not only encourage the people we address but also the people who overhear us. They show more about the condition of the heart of the person speaking them than any MRI could reveal.

Inspiration and Application

1. At the beginning of the chapter I shared about my social experiment in spreading goodwill. I verbally acknowledged and thanked the cashier for the kind interaction, and the next customer picked up on the positive attitude. Proverbs 16:24 says, "Gracious speech is like clover honey—good taste to the soul, quick energy to the

body." Make a list of five places you frequent where you could impact the associates and other customers with Wonder Words. Take your children with you to conduct your experiment so they can see how it works.

2. Proverbs 25:15 teaches, "Patient persistence pierces through indifference; gentle speech breaks down rigid defenses." Based on this verse, what three character traits must we demonstrate in order to break down our children's rigid defenses so that Wonder Words naturally flow out of their hearts?

3. If we want the use of Wonder Words to be second nature for our children, it has to be first nature to us. As the habit is developing, our children will only use them about _____ percent of the time that we do.

4. Wonder Words have the biggest impact when we use them in complete sentences. In your sentence, it's nice to include the other person's name and say what you're thanking her for, asking for, or apologizing for. For practice, write a sentence thanking Sara for picking up Joshua, your son, from art class this afternoon. Write a sentence asking your neighbor Jonathan if you and your husband can please borrow his wheelbarrow for some yard work you're doing Saturday. Finally, write a sentence apologizing to Kate for being 20 minutes late to the planning committee meeting. After you're comfortable with this exercise, try it verbally with your children around the dinner table, using scenarios they are likely to encounter.

5. What is probably the most overlooked Wonder Word (or phrase), and why is it an asset to our vocabulary?

10

Gracious Hosts
and Great Guests

*The ornaments of your house will be
the guests who frequent it.*

UNKNOWN

Etiquette IQ Quiz

1. When is the most gracious time to RSVP to an invitation?

   A. within 24 hours of receiving the invitation

   B. within one week of receiving the invitation

   C. anytime before the "respond by" date listed on the invitation

2. The invitation states that the children's party begins at four o'clock. What time would be best to arrive at the host's home?

   A. three fifty

   B. four o'clock

   C. four ten

3. As the host of a playdate you should...

   A. let the guest choose the activities

   B. let the guest choose from several activities you have pre-planned

   C. have a preplanned activity and allow the guest to choose from some other activities if time permits*

Answers: 1) A 2) C 3) C.*

113

The guard opened the gate and allowed us entrance into the exclusive neighborhood of millionaires, movie stars, and sports heroes. As soon as we pulled up to the estate, we knew this was going to be unlike any birthday party we had ever attended—let alone for a five-year-old.

Lining the mansion's driveway was a welcoming menagerie of performers, friendly clowns, and jugglers. As we walked under a massive arch of balloons, smiling faces in circus attire invited us to the bounty of the hot-dog wagon, ice-cream truck, and popcorn and cotton-candy carts. Marc (holding a blue cone of spun sugar), Kent, and I were awed as a stilt walker tipped his hat to us and said, "Please, follow me to the party!"

He led us through a gate into the back lawn. There we were greeted by two white ponies decked out to look like unicorns. The laughter of children running in the plush lawn, jumping in bounce houses, and climbing a rock wall added to the dreamlike carnival atmosphere.

Marc and the birthday girl met in Sunday school and were smitten with each other from the first time they shared crayons. Now wearing a birthday princess hat, she spotted Marc and came running up to him. He smiled, swallowed his too-big bite of cotton candy, and said, "Happy birthday, Whitney! Thank you for inviting me to your party."

I smiled, half in relief and half in disbelief. Our preparty practice had paid off!

Our introverted, self-conscious, strong-willed, and serious firstborn had risen to the occasion to greet his hostess with more than the usual, "hey." Whitney's parents were two steps behind her. He greeted them kindly too. With that, he handed me his cotton candy and ran off with Whitney into a bounce house—a miniature version of the circus big top.

During the party Marc joined in, played nicely with the other children, and happily watched Whitney open her gifts. With the last present unwrapped, it was time for the surprise grand finale of the party. Suddenly, music that had played quietly in the background was turned up, a DJ appeared, and a dance floor that I had barely noticed before lit up. The floor began to flash in dizzy patterns of red, blue, and yellow. The DJ invited all the children to come show everyone their best moves in a dance-off!

All the children leaped onto the dance floor. All of them, that is, except Marc.

Knowing him, I assumed immediately that he would be mortified. He doesn't so much as tap his foot. Fully dancing in public was *not* going to happen. I turned to see his reaction, but he was gone. I tapped Kent on the shoulder. "Where is he?" I asked.

We went looking in separate directions. I found him at the top of the rock-climbing wall.

"Marc, sweetie, come down. Whitney is having a dance contest," I said, looking up to his high hiding place, my hand to my forehead to shield the midday sun from my eyes.

"No way, Mommy. I'm not dancing!"

"You don't have to dance, Marc. But you need to join in by watching. It's rude to disregard the contest that Whitney and her parents planned and do your own thing."

"I can't go over there, Mommy. Dancing hurts my head."

His remark was so desperate and so cute. I wanted to chuckle, but I held it back and offered him reassurance instead.

"Marc, Daddy and I will stand beside you. We'll all watch together. No one will make you dance. Now come on down so we can rejoin everyone."

"Yes, ma'am," he said in resignation as he started his deliberately slow descent.

We took a place in the back of the crowd of parents gathered around the dance floor. At first, Marc could barely look in the direction of the dancing. He glanced longingly at the rock wall several times. Then, pulled in by the laughter of the children dancing and the applause of the adult onlookers, he began to relax. A smile replaced his previously fearful expression.

"You're doing great watching everyone, sweetie," I told him.

"Thank you, Mommy. It's hard not doing what I want, but I know that I'm doing what Whitney would want. So I guess that's better."

"You're kind and thoughtful. I like that about you," I whispered encouragingly to him.

"Thanks, Mommy." He beamed back.

At that moment they started handing $20 bills at random to the children on the dance floor as prizes. I couldn't help but think that Marc was probably experiencing the most extravagant party of his life. I wondered if he'd even remember it in a few years. The other day I asked him about it. He doesn't recall the day.

Though the party didn't become a lasting memory for him, it gave him a chance to practice some of the traits of being a great guest. He exercised his social muscles, and they became stronger for it. They were able to carry him further at the next event, and the next… He's grown in graciousness as he's grown in years. When our children do that, we have more than enough reason to celebrate!

So Many Opportunities

Parties, playdates, sleepovers…as our children are growing up, they have many opportunities to be hosts or guests. The learned behaviors that make our children gracious hosts and great guests help them set aside their momentary wants and desires to consider other people's. These behaviors help our children become confident in their social skills and kind and thoughtful in their actions. Etiquette alone is not likely to turn a wallflower into the life of the party, but of course, that's not what we're after. Our goal isn't to change our children into something other than what Christ created them to be. Rather, we want to show them the how-to's of great interpersonal skills. This will guide them as they grow into the most Christ-honoring version of themselves. Let's discover the essential skills for doing just that by being gracious hosts and great guests.

Information to Include in Every Invitation

Every event begins with an invitation. The card does more than share the time, date, and location of a party. The look sets the tone of the event (formal or casual) and gives your guests insights into how to dress and what to expect at the party. An invitation should include the information your guests need in order to feel prepared for what's in store when they arrive.

I've received two invitations for birthday parties that failed to mention anyone's name. Both of them came home from school in my boys' backpacks with no other identifying information but a phone number to RSVP. The invitations appeared gender neutral, so I didn't even know if I was responding for the party of a boy or girl. When I asked my sons if they knew who was having a party, they didn't know. All they said was that the teacher put the invitation in their take-home folder. Each time it took me a day or so to get a name so I could address the mom by name when I called to RSVP!

Here's the information to include on every invitation so your guests aren't left wondering.

- *The reason for the party.* Include whether this party is for a birthday, the end of school, Christmas, or such.

- *The guest of honor.* Share the first and last name of the guest of honor for birthday parties or the host for all other parties.

- *The day and date.* Write out both the day of the week and the date like this: Sunday, March 16.

- *Location.* Include the physical address and also what the location is, such as a home, restaurant, or park.

- *Start and end time.* For parties, especially where the guests are not old enough to drive themselves, both the start and end time should be noted. Children's parties generally last two hours for ages five and under. For children six and up, three hours is fine.

- *RSVP.* Share the phone number or e-mail address (or both) you would like guests to use when responding.

- *Dress.* Let guests know if you expect a certain type of dress. For instance, a girl's sixteenth birthday party might be rather formal, or it might be a relaxed afternoon by the pool. You'll want your guests to know they've come dressed for the occasion.

- *Special information.* Here's your opportunity to let guests know if it's a surprise party or if they should bring anything like a shirt to wear over their clothes for a messy craft project.

Once the invitations are ready, it's time to invite your guests!

Choosing Whom to Invite

Children will often want to invite everyone they know because more guests means more gifts. But parties aren't all about us, even when we're the guest of honor. They are opportunities to acknowledge our friends. At the party, the guest of honor needs time and energy to pay attention to each guest one-on-one at least for a few minutes. I've yet to meet a nine-year-old who can make each of the 25 other children at a party feel as if he or she is the only person in the room. The adage that the perfect number of guests is your child's age plus one makes things more manageable for young hosts and guests.

When making out the guest list, keep in mind how many helpers you'll have at the party. Make sure you can keep track of all your guests at once because as the host's mom, you're in charge of safety.

You don't have to invite the whole class, team, club, or such. Also, be careful not to invite everyone except a few children. Doing so makes those children feel like outcasts. To avoid hurt feelings, it's best to invite about 25 percent of the group. It's fine to have parties that are just for girls or just for boys, and doing so can cut your guest list in half.

Sending and Responding to Invitations

Mailing an invitation to each guest is still the best option. When invitations are sent home in backpacks, children sometimes lose them before parents have the chance to see them.

E-mailing an invitation is a less expensive alternative, but people receive so many e-mails that your invitation may be overlooked or forgotten as soon as it's read.

For children's parties, mailing invitations three to four weeks in advance is fine. If the party falls on a holiday, mail the invitations up to six weeks in advance because people make holiday plans early.

RSVP stands for the initials for the French words *repondez s'il vous plait* (pronounced ray-pon-DAY SEE voo play). The words loosely translate as "please respond." An RSVP is a request to let the host know whether the recipient will be able to accept the host's offer of hospitality. Ask guests to respond about a week in advance or however long you need to prepare for the number of guests you're expecting.

Invitation recipients should actually respond to an invitation within 24 hours of receipt. Your fast reply lets the host know you're happy to be invited and that you've given her invitation special attention. To not respond to an invitation is to ignore her.

Even if you can't attend, RSVP and let the host know your child can't make it. If the reason isn't too personal, share with the host why you're not able to attend. Responding early gives the host an opportunity to invite someone else. As a host, never ask guests why they can't attend or push for them to come. It's

Mom to Mom

Until recently, including an "RSVP by" date on an invitation was considered bad form. It implied that we didn't expect guests to be gracious enough to respond quickly on their own. Today, because people are so lax about responding, RSVP dates are standard on invitations. Unfortunately, most people don't take into account the planning that someone else needs to do in order to entertain them.

Help your child build empathy by considering together how it makes people feel as they wait and wonder whether he'll be joining them. Discuss the difficulties of food and activity planning when you're uncertain about who will be attending an event. Let your child hear you RSVP to parties so you can model for him how easy it is to say, "Thank you for the invitation to Jackson's party! José is looking forward to being there!"

kind to simply say, "Thank you for letting me know. We'll miss Tommy at the party. It will be a joy to have him join us next time."

Once the "RSVP by" date has passed, the hostess can contact guests and say something like, "I mailed an invitation to Mary Beth's end-of-school party about three weeks ago. I haven't heard from you and want to make sure you received the invitation. Are you able to join us?"

It's Your Party (Being a Gracious Host)

All gracious hosts share certain hallmarks. They're eager to put their guests at ease, see to their comfort, and make sure they're enjoying themselves as much as the host is. In general, they make their guests feel as if the special day or event wouldn't have been nearly as special without them there. This feeling is passed along through the host's actions and attitudes. Here are the hallmarks of great hosting to pass along to our children.

When Guests First Arrive

Greet your guests warmly at the door. Even pint-sized hosts should greet their guests at the door along with Mom or Dad. That way the host can say, "I'm glad you're here!" right from the start. Guests who might be nervous will feel more at ease when the friend who invited them also welcomes them. At the door the host can greet guests by welcoming them and thanking them for coming. "Hello, Jess! Thank you for coming. Please come in!"

Acknowledge gifts. If a guest has brought a gift, acknowledge the present and either take it from the guest so that her hands are free or let her know where the gift table is so she can place it there.

Offer refreshments. Even though the food might not be served until later at the party, offer your guests something to drink soon after they arrive.

Introduce guests to others. If parents haven't met the guests before, introductions should be made. Also, either lead each guest to someone she knows or introduce her to someone new so she doesn't feel alone. "Marisa and Kara from our softball team are here. Come on, I'll help you find them."

During the Party

Divide your time. At parties, junior hosts sometimes spend all their time with their best friends. Share with children that spending most of their time with just one or a few guests can make the others feel as if you invited them only for their gifts.

Participate in your own party. Children will sometimes get caught up having fun doing one thing and not take part in the activities for their own party. When I didn't see my son in the bounce house on a recent birthday, I went looking for him. I found him and two other friends playing a video game in his room.

Thank guests for coming. As guests leave, thank them for coming to the party. Also thank each child's parents for bringing them. "Thank you for coming, Leigh! Thank you for bringing her, Mrs. Rochester."

> ## *Mom to Mom*
>
> When visiting a home, don't step over the threshold until you've been invited to do so. Wait until the person opening the door says, "Please come in!" If she forgets to invite you, ask her, "May I come in?" and wait for her answer before entering.

Being a Great Guest

Being a guest entails more than just showing up. Great guests make hosts feel glad they invited them. They participate in the party, get along well with the other guests, and let hosts know they were happy to have been included.

When You First Arrive

Don't be early or late. Last-minute details often mount up for a host. For that reason it's gracious not to arrive early for a party and interrupt the preparations. Arriving five to ten minutes after the time on the invitation gives the host a few minutes to take care of things that were unforeseen or that required a little more time than she expected. Arriving more than ten minutes late keeps the host glued to the front door to welcome latecomers and unable to join the other guests.

Let your host know you're glad to be there. When the door is opened, let the host know you're glad to be there by greeting and thanking him. "Merry Christmas, Luke! Thank you for inviting me," or "Hello, Jasmine. Thank you for inviting me!" Your child should also greet and thank the host's parents.

Join in the fun. When the party switches from one activity to another, guests should follow suit. If they're not comfortable participating, they don't have to join in except by watching. However, they shouldn't disregard the host's plans by ignoring the activity to do their own thing.

During the Party

Say "thank you." You will have lots of opportunities at a party to express gratitude by saying "thank you": when you arrive, when you're offered something to eat or drink, when you are given a party favor, and when you leave. Also, if you like the food, it's nice to compliment it.

Clean up your cup and plate. Pick up your plate, cup, and anything else at your place setting and ask where you should put it.

Let an adult know if something spills. If you see a spill or notice that something is broken, let a grown-up know right away so it can be taken care of.

Shhh! No bragging. Children often want to let everyone at a party know what gift they brought. Explain to them that this is a type of bragging.

Stay with the other guests. Let children know they need to stay where the party is and not wander through a guest's home. They should ask the host or his parents where the bathroom is instead of looking for it on their own.

Especially for Playdates and Sleepovers

The skills we've already covered apply to playdates as well as parties. There are additional behaviors that will help our children better enjoy all their playdates and sleepovers too. It's best to invite children over for a playdate or two before you invite them for a sleepover. That gives you a chance to see how well they play together before committing to have the children together overnight.

When considering scheduling either a playdate or sleepover, it's nice to plan out some activities in advance. When children play often with the same child (like the next-door neighbor), no plans are needed. However, if you're inviting a child for the first time, it's nice for you and your child to plan an activity or two and build in time for free playing as well as time permits.

When you call to invite the guest, share with his mom the activities you have planned. This sets the expectations of both the host and his guest and cuts down on a lot of frustrations ("I don't want to do that"). When you call to invite your child's friend, you can say something like this: "Hello, this is Rachel, Joshua's mom. We were wondering if Lucas could come over Saturday from noon until three. We'd like him to join us for lunch, and then we thought the boys could play on the trampoline and watch the DVD of the newest Karate Kangaroos movie."

Additional Skills for Hosts and Guests

Consideration of Others

Allow the guest to choose free-time activities. Give your guest two or more options for what to play, and then allow her to choose.

Guests go first. Guests should be invited to go first and also should be served first.

Don't ignore other family members. Young guests should say hello to the host's family members and not ignore or exclude siblings who might want to join in. But guests should give most of their attention to the people who invited them.

Boundaries

Ask before helping yourself. It's fine to let the host know you're hungry or thirsty. Just make sure to ask and don't help yourself to anything unless you've been invited to do so.

Mom to Mom

When inviting a child to join you and your family, it's assumed the host will be paying. If that's not the case, to avoid confusion, be sure to make it known when you extend the invitation. If your child is the guest, it's always nice to offer to pay for some or part of the cost, especially if it's an expensive day out at an amusement park or the like. It's also kind to provide your child with money to buy his or her own souvenirs.

When your child is going to be a guest at someone else's house, explain that not every house is run just like yours. Other families might eat dinner earlier or later, allow eating only in the kitchen or dining room, have an earlier bedtime, or a multitude of other things. Guests shouldn't comment on the way the hosts run their home: "I get to stay up until 10:30 on Saturday nights. Why do we have to go to sleep now? It's only 10:00?"

Ask before opening. Don't open doors, windows, closets, or drawers unless you've been asked to do so.

Don't touch electronics. Ask before turning on the TV or using a computer, tablet, video game system, MP3 player, or any other electronic device.

Tidying Up

Clear your place setting. Offer to take your plate and other items to the sink after eating.

Wet items. Ask what to do with wet towels and clothing.

Clean up before leaving. Guests should help clean up the toys and anything else they played with before leaving.

Open Home, Open Heart

There are so many occasions in childhood to celebrate! In fact, any day is a great day to open your home, gather your family and friends, and celebrate a new day full of fresh possibilities. Each day brings opportunities to share hospitality and friendship with those who come into your home. When you do, you're opening not only your home but also your heart. Whether you're attending an extravagant event like the birthday party my family was invited to or sharing hot dogs and Diet Dr Pepper with friends on your back porch, your thoughtful fellowship makes the sweetest of memories.

Christ wants us to be in relationship with one another. The more we're in tune with what makes us gracious hosts and great guests, the more opportunities we will have to fellowship with one another. Someone once said, "The ornaments of your house will be the guests who frequent it." And who doesn't want a home decorated with the ornaments of graciousness, caring, and friendship!

Inspiration and Application

1. In Luke 7:36-50 we find the story of a sinful woman (an uninvited guest) anointing Jesus's feet during dinner in the home of a

Pharisee. The Pharisee left a lot to be desired as a host. He didn't provide any of the usual forms of hospitality shown to guests. He failed to wash Jesus's feet, which was a common first-century courtesy because feet got dirty wearing sandals. He also didn't anoint Jesus's head with oil (a type of personal blessing) or give Jesus a kiss of greeting when He arrived. Jesus knew the good manners of His day for being a gracious host and a great guest, and He followed them. Read the passage and notice how Jesus spoke to the Pharisee about his disregard for the duties of a host.

2. The customs of how we dine and welcome others into our homes have changed through the centuries, but the spirit behind the ancient and modern forms of welcoming and honoring guests has remained the same. List the ancient etiquette described in Luke 7:36-50 along with today's equivalent.

3. Knowing your child, what three skills from this chapter would help your child to be a more gracious host?

4. What three skills from this chapter would help your child be a more gracious party guest?

5. Being a host or a guest is fun, but it's also a responsibility. List three ideas from this chapter that you will model for your children as you grow in graciousness right along with them.

11

Giving and Receiving Gifts Gleefully

The only gift is a portion of thyself.
RALPH WALDO EMERSON

Etiquette IQ Quiz

1. For children's birthday parties, the gifts should be opened...

   A. during the party

   B. after the party

   C. at the party if it's held in a home, after the party if it's held in a public place

2. Two of your child's friends give him the same video game. When he opens the second one, he should say to the friend who gave it to him...

   A. "Thank you! Now I have one to play with and one to share."

   B. "Thank you! I'll exchange it for another game that's similar."

   C. "Thank you! My mom and I will exchange it for something else."

3. When you are the recipient of a gift in the mail, you should...

   A. Call and let the giver know it arrived even if you're not opening it until the special day.

B. Open it right away so you can thank the giver.

C. Wait until the day when you open the gift and then send the giver a thank-you note when you send out your other thank-you notes.*

Christmas came just 12 weeks after Kent and I were married.

I envisioned a perfect little Christmas morning for us. I didn't even care about what I would get for Christmas (or so I thought).

Sitting on the floor next to the tree, I picked up the largest gift first. It was wrapped in shiny, navy-blue paper and packed so full that dozens of strips of tape barely kept the lid in place. "I wrapped it myself if you can't tell," Kent said sheepishly.

I smiled.

I cut through the last piece of tape and pulled off the lid.

Before me was a red plaid flannel shirt. Under it was a pair of black corduroy pants. Any lumberjack would have been proud to call the outfit his own.

It was the least likely thing I would ever wear. And yet this was what my husband bought me. In a sudden panic I wondered, is this how he saw me?

I muttered a thank-you.

I tried to shake off my disappointment, anger, and confusion, but I didn't hide my feelings well.

He was heartbroken and had not meant to hurt me. He didn't like the clothes either, but the lady in the fashionable store where he bought them told him it was all the rage. She assured him that I would love this new look. He had never been married before and was new at buying his wife Christmas gifts.

We talked. All was understood. Yet still, all these years later, I can feel the intensity of my reaction, my questioning, and my heartbreak that wanted to scream out, "You don't know me at all! And that's what I want most—for you to know me, and in your knowing, to love me more for it."

Answers: 1) A 2) A 3) A.

Two Parts of Every Gift

Why is giving or receiving a gift so memorable? A gift has two parts: the object itself and the emotions that go with it. The emotional part impacts us the most. That's why the old saying rings true: It's not the gift that counts, it's the thought. When a gift is not thoughtful, it can leave us sad or upset. On the other hand, we remember and appreciate other gifts because of the thought that went into them.

What are the three best gifts your child has ever received? What are your own three favorite presents? I'll bet each one was special because the gift was so very "you" or because it was a beautiful reflection of the other person's love for you.

A package arrived in the mail for me the other day. It was the sweetest type of gift, one given "just because" from a friend, and it included this note: "I saw these in the store and thought of you. They're very 'Maralee.' Enjoy!" My precious friend knows I adore anything with birds. When I lifted the cotton padding in the gift box, I found five little figurines—a blue and yellow mama bird with four baby birds. They are precious to my heart because they remind me that I have a friend who knows me well.

It's Even Harder for Children

If receiving a gift that doesn't hit the mark is emotionally difficult for us moms, consider how much our children will struggle to handle this gracefully. If Great-Grandma gives Elmo blocks to our eight-year-old for her birthday, our daughter's first thought isn't naturally "Thank you for thinking of me." She's more likely to think something like this: "I'm embarrassed. I just opened this in front of my friends. Elmo is for three-year-olds. People are going to think I like baby stuff!" If our 14-year-old unwraps a football video game but wanted an alien-themed one, he's going to think, "Are you crazy? This game isn't any fun." When we don't connect emotionally with a present, we have a hard time showing appreciation.

That's why it's a good idea to explain to our children the two parts to every gift. When they understand this, they can better handle the emotional ups and downs that come with opening Christmas and birthday gifts. It's also a fundamental step, one too often overlooked, in teaching our children the art of choosing gifts for others with careful and loving thought.

Prepare Your Child to Receive Gifts

We wish our children would express thankfulness as freely as they express dissatisfaction, but it's especially hard for them to slow down enough to express gratitude in the middle of the tinsel-strewn excitement of Christmas or the cake-and-crepe-paper fun of birthdays. Here's how to help prepare them.

Remind children what "thank you" means. Most children aren't clear about the definition of "thank you." It doesn't mean "I love this!" or even "I like this." It means "I notice you did something for me." Children often feel as if saying "thank you" is telling a fib if the gift they just opened isn't something they adore. When they understand that saying "thank you" has nothing to do with how much they like or don't like what they're thanking the other person for, they're more apt to say—and mean it.

Talk about the feeling. Talk to your child about how he feels when people appreciate something special he did and how he feels when no one seems to notice. Explain that every time he says "thank you," he is giving someone the good feeling of being regarded and appreciated.

Practice the four Ps— Practice Prevents Poor Parties. In the days leading up

---

✑*Mom to Mom*

Nothing succeeds like success! If your child has had a successful experience of opening gifts graciously, she'll be able to rise to the occasion the next time. That's why role-playing opening gifts a day or so before a party is such a good idea. It gives your child success to build on. To role-play, actually wrap up some things around the house, including something that your child would find embarrassing (underwear from when they were little will do the trick every time!), two of the same item, and something that she would find less than fun. No one likes to be caught not knowing what to say, so as you unwrap these "surprises," you can give your child gracious words she can use in awkward situations to make herself and others more at ease.

to a party, role-play with your children so they know what to do if they open a gift they don't like. It isn't necessary to fib and say they love it. However, they should acknowledge the gift giver by smiling, making eye contact, and saying something like this: "Thank you, Uncle Mark! You're always kind to buy me a present."

Avoid the "Open and Disregard" Syndrome. Role-play with your child so he knows how to slow down and say "thank you" after opening each gift. "Thank you for the video game, Uncle Shane! This is the one I've wanted for months." Teaching your child to thank the giver before going on to the next gift prevents the "open and disregard" syndrome that happens when children tear open packages without paying attention to the gift or showing gratitude to the giver.

Growing in Graciousness
(Next-Level Skills)

Dealing with Gifts You Can't Use

> Together with your child, decide in advance what you'll do with duplicate gifts or things that you know he won't enjoy playing with. If a child knows in advance that if Great-Grandma gives him a "little kid" gift again this year, you'll donate it to the children's ward of the hospital, exchange it for something else, or give it to the three-year-old next door, he'll feel less disappointment. (Remind him before the party that he doesn't need to tell people what he plans to do with their gift after the party!)

Opening Gifts

It's good manners to open gifts at the party whether the party is held at home or in a public place. The giver has gone to all the trouble of shopping for your gift, wrapping it, and bringing it to the party. He should get to see you open it and your appreciation in person. Gifts are opened during bridal and baby showers for the same reason. Here are some basics that can be applied at almost any age, though your littlest ones will need help reading the cards.

Open the card first. Children are excited to get right to the gift. When they open the card first, they exercise self-control and show that the giver is more important to them than the gift.

Say the name of the gift giver out loud, but don't read the message out loud. When you open the card, look for the name of the gift giver first, and announce it to the group. "This gift is from Ashley." While people's attention is momentarily focused on Ashley, read the card silently (because those sentiments are private). Then you may make a brief comment for the benefit of the person who gave the card: "Thank you for the beautiful card," or "You picked out such a nice card." If your child is too young to read, read the card quietly to him or her.

Make sure the giver is in the room before opening the gift. Sometimes at parties, the gift giver might be in another room during some of the gift opening. Someone should ask the person to come into the room before his or her gift is opened.

Say something nice about the gift before opening the next one. Take a few moments to look at the gift and share something about it that you like or find interesting. "The Lego set has three mini-figurines with it—they're my favorites!" or "This mini tea set has pretty yellow and purple flowers!"

Say "thank you" in a complete sentence. Simply saying "thanks" or "thank you" isn't enough. Express your gratitude by at least using a complete sentence, including the person's name. "This Alien Mutant Space Race game is going to be fun, Sheri. Thank you!"

If you receive identical gifts, don't show disappointment with the second one. When you open an identical gift, thank the giver and realize he is probably feeling bad that his gift was a duplicate. It's best to thank the person and decide privately what you want to do with the duplicate gift. Often it's fun to have two of the same gift. "Thank you, Kevin. Now I have one for home and one to keep at my grandmother's house."

Keep the gift in its box. Wait until after the party before playing with a particular item. Taking each toy out of its packaging, undoing all the secure ties, and installing batteries is time-consuming. It will make the gift-opening process take too long for onlookers.

Write down the gift-givers' names. A parent or other adult should make

> ## *Mom to Mom*
>
> When a gift arrives in the mail, it's nice to contact the giver to acknowledge that the gift arrived safely. Calling is nice because the other person gets to hear the sound of your voice, but even a text message is better than not acknowledging a gift's arrival.

a note of each gift and the giver's name. We might think we'll be able to remember who gave what at a small party. But even with five or six guests, it's easy to get confused. We wouldn't want to thank someone for the wrong gift.

Great Giving

When your child is not the birthday boy or girl, you have the opportunity to teach generosity and thoughtfulness as you select a gift for someone else. There's more to giving a gift than taking a trip to the toy aisle. For children it involves putting themselves in another's shoes, which does not come naturally. Here are two principles to remember when considering what to bring.

Take a gift. A children's birthday party invitation requires a gift from all who attend. No gift is needed if your child doesn't attend the party unless the birthday child gave a gift to your child on her last birthday or if the gift is for a best friend or relative. Writing "no gifts, please" on invitations to adult parties is fine, but not with children's parties. The reason is that only about half of your guests will follow your request and not bring a gift. Those who don't bring one will feel bad when they see that so many people did. If your child would like to donate gifts received, make a note on the invitation: "Gifts are being donated to the Westwood Children's Home."

Tailor the gift to the recipient. It's often hard for children to look outside themselves and pick out something based solely on what the other person would like. Guide your child in the right direction. "I know baseball is your favorite sport. Is it Luke's too? I seem to remember him saying he liked basketball. Do you know what his favorite team is? We could get him a team ball."

Outstanding Observation

When your child is a guest at another's party, he will need patience, generosity of spirit, and self-control to sit and happily watch someone else receive gifts. Here are some guidelines you can give your child before the party so he knows how to help the guest of honor enjoy a special day.

Don't ask for your gift to be opened next. Unless you're leaving the party early, don't ask for your gift to be opened next.

Don't announce to others what you gave. When your gift is opened and after it's been opened, don't brag to others about the gift you gave.

Don't ask the recipient whether he likes the gift. It's hard not to wonder, but asking could force the other person not to tell the truth. In addition, the question itself takes attention away from the other guests and the party in general and puts attention on the person who gave the gift.

Don't offer to help unwrap. Part of the fun of special days is unwrapping the gifts. Unless the guest of honor asks for help, don't offer to help him unwrap their gifts.

Don't ask if you can play with a gift. Toys should not be taken out of their boxes until after the party. Don't put the birthday boy in the awkward position of saying no.

Try not to be jealous. It's hard for a lot of children not to want the things their friends have. Let your child know that after the party, he can tell you about anything he saw that he would like for his next birthday, but that during the party, he shouldn't say, "Oh man! I so want that!"

"A Portion of Thyself"

Gift giving and receiving is about more than what's wrapped in the box. The actual gift carries with it emotions that are often remembered and felt long after the gift has been opened. We bless our children by helping them grow in graciousness when we teach them that with gifts, it's the thought that counts, and that loving thought makes every gift more special—whether we're on the giving or receiving end.

Inspiration and Application

1. "Every desirable and beneficial gift comes out of heaven. The gifts are rivers of light cascading down from the Father of Light. There is nothing deceitful in God, nothing two-faced, nothing fickle" (James 1:17). We are blessed by God with glorious gifts. How should this affect the way we give to others?

2. We all know stories of people who did not follow the example of James 1:17. Instead, they gave gifts insincerely—to win people's favor or influence them. How can we address this with our children so they realize the difference between giving a gift to honor a friendship and giving one to appease someone or gain a friend?

3. Gifts should be opened at the party, so how many guests do you think should be invited to your child's next party in order for all the gifts to be opened in twenty minutes (for older children) or ten minutes (for children less than five years old)?

4. List four items from around your home that you can wrap and use with your child when role-playing about how to graciously open gifts. Include an item that is silly or embarrassing, two of the same item wrapped individually (duplicate gifts), and a gift that just isn't something she finds fun or interesting. How will practicing in advance better prepare her for the emotions involved with receiving gifts?

5. Help your child experience the joy of giving. Decide together who you will surprise with a gift, think about the perfect gift for her, and give it "just because." How did this process help your child understand the joy of giving?

12

Growing in Gratitude

*Gratitude bestows reverence....changing
forever how we experience life and the world.*
JOHN MILTON

Etiquette IQ Quiz

1. In the first line of a thank-you card, you should...

   A. include the words *thank you*

   B. pay the giver a compliment

   C. mention the gift by name

2. Is a written thank-you note necessary if you opened the gift and thanked the giver in person?

   A. It's necessary.

   B. It's nice but not necessary.

   C. It's necessary only if the gift was expensive or difficult to come by.

3. With modern manners, an e-mail thank-you note expresses your thanks as fully as a handwritten note.

   A. sometimes

   B. always

   C. never*

Answers: 1) B 2) B 3) A*.

Some people live a joy-filled life. Others wander through life searching for a key to happiness that eludes them. The two groups are the "haves" and the "have-nots" of the treasure of joy. What do some possess and others long for—the key that unlocks gladness and sets it free to settle in our hearts?

Gratitude.

Expressing thanks is more than a social obligation. It's the key to a life of joy. Being happy or unhappy in life has little to do with money, the size of your home, the brand of your car, or the locales of your vacations. The happiest people I know always talk about their blessings, even when their current circumstances are not good. On the other hand, the unhappiest people I know, despite their circumstances, instinctively tell you about their problems.

For the "haves," joy has arrived. For the "have-nots," joy's arrival has been delayed by worries, unmet expectations, or unfulfilled wants. Each day brings new disappointments that keep joy just out of reach—close enough to see and envy but too far away to grasp.

We are not naturally content; we tend to reach out for more. We say to ourselves, "Joy will come in the morning." However, until we count the blessings already in our hands and hold them to our hearts, joy will always be a day away.

Our children will spend their lives chasing fantasies if we don't teach them how to count everything as blessing and joy today and model that skill ourselves. An extensive study conducted by the University of California found that youth who are ungrateful are "less satisfied with life." As these children grow up, they are more likely than others to "be aggressive and engage in risk-taking behaviors, such as early or frequent promiscuous activities, substance use...and poor habits."[1]

How to Begin

Your children will more easily embrace the verbal and written forms of gratitude when they see and hear your happy habit of expressing them. A good way to do this is to tell your children how grateful you are for them.

For eight years I constantly said to my son Corbett something like this: "I'm so glad you're my son. I thank Jesus for you today." For eight years, his response was mostly silence. One day in the car last year he said, "Mommy, I'm thankful you're my mom." Since then, several times a week he'll spontaneously express his appreciation, gratitude, or love for me, for his dad, and for his brother.

The other morning he told 15-year-old Marc, "You're the best brother ever."

Marc smiled and replied, "No, you're the best brother ever. I'm the second best."

As they laughed, I turned my head to hide my tears of gladness. It's taken eight years, but I now have a nine-year-old who is getting into the habit of expressing gratitude. Each time he does it, his face lights with joy from within.

> ## ℳom to ℳom
>
> You can display gifts of gratitude on a bulletin board in your kitchen or family room. Using decorative paper, sticky notes, or index cards, encourage family members to write down one thing they're grateful for. As the board fills with gratitude notes, it's a lovely visual of all your family has been blessed with. The more notes you and your children write, the more you'll all begin to recognize gifts of graciousness that previously went unnoticed.

Sprinkle your daily conversations with gratitude for all your blessings. You could say, "I was thinking today of how grateful I am that Mrs. Bowlin lives next door," or "We're so blessed to have peanut butter. We like it so much, and it tastes good."

Nothing is too small to mention. Lead the way by keeping a list or journal of what you're thankful for, share it with your family, and ask them to add to it.

Thank Others at the Next Point of Contact

Much of this chapter will be devoted to thank-you notes—tangible expressions of your appreciation. However, don't overlook the importance of thanking the person the very next time you come into contact with her.

Regardless of what form the contact takes—e-mail, text, instant chat, phone conversation, or so on—say a few words of appreciation. For example, if your friend treats you to lunch and you talk to her on the phone the next day, be sure to express your gratitude again at that time. You can still send a handwritten note after that. The main thing is to remember to mention the person's kindness the next time you connect.

In this chapter about gratitude, you will learn how to teach your children about verbal and written forms of gratitude, including...

the gold standard of gratitude: the handwritten note

electronic expressions of gratitude—when are they okay?

the four-step formula for writing treasured thank-you notes

occasions for sending thank-you notes

time frames for sending thank-you notes

how to instill this habit—from toddler to teen

incorporating gratitude in your daily dialogue

The Gold Standard of Gratitude: The Handwritten Note

I doubt anyone is ever going to open a handwritten thank-you note, read it, and say to their spouse, "Honey, would you look at this! Gillian wrote me a thank-you note just to say it was nice to see me and she appreciated me buying her coffee last Saturday. What a waste of time and a stamp!"

Gratitude doesn't offend people, and hand-addressed mail is a treat. If either of my boys goes to the mailbox and finds a hand-addressed envelope in it, he'll coming running to me saying, "Mom, someone sent us a card! Can I open it?" We'll look at the handwriting and try to guess who it's from, and then he'll open it and read it aloud. Then we'll lay the card on the counter for Kent to read when he gets home.

A handwritten note is special because it's one of the few forms of communication that carries the sender's DNA. It's truly personal. It's forever marked with her unique handwriting and sealed with her own hands. The hands-on touch makes it special, like a hug sent through the mail. Often the card is kept for days or weeks. If the words are especially meaningful, the recipient might put it in a box of cards she keeps forever. I have a box like that, and every word within it is precious to me. When you want your gratitude to have the longest shelf (heart) life, send a handwritten note.

Electronic Expressions of Gratitude— When Are They Okay?

Five years ago if someone asked me whether he should e-mail a note of thanks, my answer would have been a pleasant but firm no. However, because etiquette evolves to meet our changing sensibilities and technology, the answer is now yes...sometimes. Here are my guidelines for electronic expressions of gratitude.

People you don't know face-to-face. If you only know someone through a virtual environment, thank her through that environment. Stepping out of it to thank her in a more personal way might make her feel awkward, as if you've stalked her to find her home or work address. There are exceptions of course. Several people I first met on Facebook are now good friends. However, practice safety first; never allow your child or teen to do this.

Facebook and Twitter. You don't want to thank someone for his gift or kindness by posting your appreciation on his Facebook wall. "Thank you for the three new books you picked out for me. They arrived today, and I look forward to..." His other friends or family members who didn't receive the same attention might be offended.

Stealing their thunder. Allow others to share their good news online before you congratulate them. You don't want to beat someone to their own big announcement and leave their other friends feeling left out. I wrote a congratulations posting on a friend's Facebook wall just hours after her first baby was born last year. I called the baby by name and said how it would be a joy to meet him in person, hold, and hug him. Unfortunately, she had not yet shared his name publicly. I had insider information from her and without thinking let others know what was hers to announce. Thankfully, I quickly realized my mistake and was able to delete my posting.

What if I'm out of stamps? Text messages are forgotten in a matter of seconds. E-mails are often overlooked or forgotten in minutes. Unless you're thanking someone for a small kindness ("Thanks for picking up Dustin's homework today"), you're better off to call or write. At least in a voice mail the other person can hear your tone of voice. This helps deliver your message with more heart than a quick text can. (By the way, you can purchase stamps and have them delivered to your home by visiting the post office website at www.USPS.com.)

The Four-Step Formula for Writing Treasured Notes

I read an article about several friends who happened to compare the thank-you notes they received. They were identical. After all the time, care, and money someone spent picking out, wrapping, and delivering a gift, why did the recipient put so little care into showing gratitude? Sometimes, sadly, it is because she feels entitled. "It's my birthday; of course people should give me gifts!" Sometimes she simply didn't know what to write. Schools don't teach Fundamentals of Thank-You Notes in fifth grade. Maybe they should.

I've found that you can often help a child want to write thank-you notes by giving her a simple formula to follow as she writes. The formula below helps anyone create truly gracious messages because it places the emphasis on the other person, on his kindness, and on the relationship you share. This formula for notes will make the joy and gratitude you're feeling obvious and touch the heart of the giver.

1. Compliment the person who gave you the gift. Keep the focus on his kindness. Don't use the word *I* because it puts the focus on you. "I had the best time yesterday at your..."

2. Write the words *thank you* and gratefully mention a detail of the gift or kind act.

3. Explain how you'll use the gift or how you enjoyed or benefited from the person's kindness.

4. Mention the next time you hope to see or connect with the other person. This shows you're glad he is in your life and you look forward to future times together.

Here are two sample notes your child (with your help) or teen might write. You'll see that if you follow the four-step formula, people of any age can write heartfelt, other-centered notes.

September 1, 2015

Dear Alex,

You know how to pick the best presents! Thank you for my new video game. I've wanted Space Ninja Battle Plan for months. The graphics are incredible. It's my new favorite! Your game is getting lots of use. My dad and I have already played twice. Tonight my mom said she even wants to give it a try with me.

I hope you can come over after school on Thursday. It will be fun to play the game together. Thank you again!

Your friend,
Shawn

October 1, 2012

Dear Mrs. Wilkes,

You are so kind to always treat me like family. Thank you for taking me to a movie and dinner with you and Janie last night.

I've wanted to see Teen Queen since I first saw the previews on TV. And Pasta Palace is one of my favorite restaurants. I really enjoyed the lasagna and breadsticks.

I look forward to seeing you when you pick up Janie at our house next week. Thank you again!

Sincerely,
Katy

Ways to Send Thank-You Notes

For party gifts. When we're opening multiple gifts, we don't have the time to pay full attention to the gift or the giver. We can express our appreciation more fully in a written thank-you note or by following up by phone or video chat.

When you appreciate someone. Thank-you notes are handwritten gifts that you can use to honor others. Give them to people who positively impact your days: your doctor, nurse, mechanic, pastor or priest, neighbor, friend, relative, children's teachers, favorite barista, and grocery store cashier. Send notes to unknown members of our armed forces serving overseas and to police officers and firefighters in your town.

Face-to-face. If you've said "thank you" in person, on a video chat, or over the phone, you don't need to follow up with a card. The recipient was able to hear the full expression of appreciation in your voice, and the conversation was able to ebb and flow in real time when it needed to. Of course, if you want, you can still follow up with a card as a permanent keepsake of your gratitude.

When to Send Thank-You Notes

I'm often asked, "How long do I have to send a thank-you note?" The question makes me sad—the person really wants to know how long she can put it off.

I picture a man down on one knee, asking the love of his life to marry him. Instead of an immediate, "Yes! I'll marry you!" she asks without emotion, "How long do I have to get back to you with an answer?" She obviously isn't thrilled or certain about their future together. A quick answer is a sure answer in this case.

So it is with thank-you notes. The more promptly you express thanks, the more the gesture is a genuine outpouring of your gratitude and not a chore. We don't put off what we really want to do.

Here are the general guidelines for how soon you need to send a thank-you card.

- For individual gifts, a card should be sent the next day.

- For birthday parties that require you to write multiple cards, a week to ten days is fine. (Don't invite more guests than you or your child can write notes to in that length of time.)

- For special occasions, such as being someone's guest at dinner, a movie, a theme park, a playdate, or the like, the card should be sent the next day.

People have asked me when it's too late to send a card. I say that it's never too late to do a nice thing. Begin your note by apologizing. "This note has taken much too long for me to send to you. For that I am sorry..." and then continue by thanking the person.

Instilling This Habit from Toddler to Teen

People treasure thank-you notes they receive from children because they are so rare in today's society. When your children embrace this courtesy as a habit, they will stand out as gracious and thoughtful people. Here is how you can train them, starting before they are even old enough to write.

Young children. Have your child next to you while you write the thank-you note for your toddler. Read what you're writing to your child and have him scribble a little picture or "write" his name on the card. Then walk excitedly to the mailbox together to send the card and talk about how happy the recipient will be to receive it.

Children who can write. These children will likely enjoy drawing on the card more than writing the note, so explain to them that their drawing is a type of thank-you. Ask them to draw a picture of themselves enjoying the gift. You can help them figure out what to say and write the words for them.

Tweens and teens. Kids this age don't like to have things sprung on them. If you and your teen are new to writing thank-you notes, don't expect him to be enthusiastic. It will feel "lame" to him.

To soften his heart, explain that you were wrong not to write notes yourself and wrong not to teach him how to as well. Let him know that you realize the importance of it now and that you want to correct this oversight in your life and in his. As he writes his note, think of a note of your own and write side by side.

Sometimes your teen may not want to write a note simply because he doesn't know what to say. Show him the simple four-step formula on page 142. When he complains that it will take "forever," tell him you know he can do it in five minutes or less and set a timer. It's a thank-you note, not a novel.

Don't take no for an answer. Take away his favorite electronic device, or don't let him see friends this weekend until the note is written. Doing so will probably get him to write the card. It might not be heartfelt, but at least it's written, and that's the first step. The heartfelt part will come in time (it might be several years) as he watches your lifestyle of gratitude bring you joy and gentleness.

Gratitude is gender neutral. A boy who doesn't express gratitude and write thank-you notes will grow into a man who doesn't thank his wife as freely and frequently as he should. This same man will have his wife pick out her future birthday and Mother's Day cards! Boys should be taught the art of expressing thanks as diligently as girls.

Incorporating Gratitude into Your Daily Dialogue

Sources of gladness are wonderful things to mention in your daily dialogue. Carrying a childhood habit of gratitude into adulthood is much easier than developing it later. If a child complains about having to write a card, she doesn't need to have the gift until the card is written. Children who "had" to write thank-you notes when they were nine usually do so out of habit (if nothing else) when they're twenty-nine and thirty-nine.

Talk about the cards you send and receive. Keep thank-you cards out so they become staples in your home, just like the salt and pepper on the kitchen table or soap on the bathroom counter—things that are common, expected, and used often.

Take your children shopping and let them pick out their own set of thank-you cards or purchase blank ones and allow them to decorate their own.

A Life Saved by Gratitude

Several years ago, an acquaintance invited me and four other guests to a ladies' Sunday brunch at her home. The beautiful handmade invitation, the flower centerpiece, the sweet necklace party favors, and the menu all seemed to be right out of *Southern Lady* magazine. It was the sweetest and yet the most elegant meal of my life. I will always remember it as a beautiful afternoon of friendship and fellowship.

The next day I wrote the hostess a thank-you note. Something told me to mention every detail and let her know how she had made a lovely memory I'd hold dear forever. When she received the card, she called me in tears. She was so touched. She said she always felt like a failure. No one else seemed to say much about her brunch, and she had put her all into it. She feared it was proof that her best wasn't good enough. She told me, "I was about to do something silly when your note arrived and changed my mind. I'll never be able to thank you enough for your thank-you note."

Shortly after the brunch, her husband was transferred to another state, and we lost contact before our friendship had time to bloom.

Sometime later, I received a phone call from a mutual friend asking for prayer for my acquaintance. She was in serious condition in the hospital. She had tried to commit suicide while her children were in school. Her husband forgot his cell phone that morning and came home unexpectedly before lunch to get it. Had he not forgotten his phone, she would be gone. The words she shared through her tears on the phone that day eerily echoed in my heart: "I was about to do something silly." I will always wonder, was her life saved that day by gratitude?

Joy is the child of gratitude, and those who have it count their blessings instead of their needs. Speak gratitude freely, frequently, and fluently, and contentment and joy will become hallmarks of your home.

Inspiration and Application

1. Philippians 4:4-6 (NIV) includes the directive, "Let your gentleness be evident to all." Why do you think Paul says this?

2. In the same verses Paul also says, "With thanksgiving, present your requests to God." Before we ask God for something, we're to thank Him for some of our blessings. How does counting our blessings help us praise God? How might thankfulness give us insight into His plans and purposes for our past, current, and even future circumstances?

3. How can you make sure that you and your family will count your blessings and express your gratitude freely, frequently, and fluently in your home?

4. Read James 1:2-3. How will you start today to consider everything with joy?

5. After talking with your children about the connection between gratitude and joy, help each child write a thank-you note to someone special.

13

Bathroom and Bodily Noise Etiquette...Oh My!

*When a child is locked in the bathroom
with water running and he says he's doing nothing,
but the dog is barking, call 9-1-1.*
ERMA BOMBECK

Etiquette IQ Quiz

1. In the past, when people didn't have a tissue with them and needed to cough or sneeze, they were advised to cover their mouths or noses with their hands. The latest recommendations from doctors advise us to...

   A. Make a fist with our left hand and cough or sneeze into the portion where our thumb encircles our first two fingers.

   B. Cough or sneeze into the crook of our elbow.

   C. Cough or sneeze into our shoulder.

2. If you're with a friend who passes gas and then says, "Excuse me," what's the most gracious way to respond to him or her?

   A. Say, "That's okay, it happens to all of us."

   B. Try to keep the mood light by saying something like "Better you than me today!"

   C. Don't say anything. Just acknowledge his or her comment with a slight smile and a nod of your head that signals you understand and continue with the conversation without directly referring to it.

3. When someone near you sneezes multiple times, how many times should you say "Bless you" or "God bless you"?

A. two times

B. three times

C. neither of the above*

I know that burps and...how should I say this?..."bodily noises released from our hither regions" aren't normal topics in etiquette books. In fact, writing a whole chapter on bathroom and bodily noise etiquette makes me feel a little on edge. I'm not uptight, but it isn't a topic I discuss eagerly. So why did I choose it?

I didn't. The topic chose me.

For five years I was a weekly guest on a popular morning radio show. One humid Florida morning, the song set was finishing, and the producers were about to cut to my first interview segment of the hour. Even though it was only eight o'clock in the morning, the temperature was already in the eighties. That day the subject for "Monday Morning Manners with Maralee" was pool etiquette, a timely August topic.

As the final song was finishing, off the air one of the cohosts accidentally burped, and then for fun he pretended to burp again—and then once more for good measure. The other host couldn't let it slide. The two of them kidded each other back and forth, and one of them said, "Maralee, there needs to be etiquette for burps and other bodily noises!"

I winked, smiled, and said, "There is!"

Within seconds the song ended, the "live" button light flicked on, and the male host looked at me with a Cheshire cat grin. I felt my eyes widen and my body go stiff. I can only imagine that my face turned geisha white. I thought, "Oh no! He's not really going to ask me about it on the air, is he?"

Sure enough, he asked! "Maralee, this is off today's subject, but I just have to know. What's the etiquette for what to say if you or the person you're with burps or...you know, worse?"

What could I do? I had no choice but to answer my friends in the radio booth, who were doubled over trying to hide their laughter, while tens of thousands of people eavesdropped on our conversation. Anxious to put the subject behind us and move on to pool etiquette, I gave a brief answer, sharing that when someone burps they can say, "Excuse me, please." The person who overhears the burp doesn't need to say anything. If he wants to put the other person at ease, he could say, "Certainly!" or "Sure, it happens to everyone." And concerning the other bodily noise, I explained that it was a social unmentionable. No one should acknowledge it in any manner—just as if it never happened. That approach usually helps everyone feel less embarrassed.

As soon as I answered his question on the air, the phone lines lit up like a pyrotechnic display. Then the line lights started blinking, which meant even more calls were coming in behind each of the lines. Twenty-four calls and counting. I panicked. "Oh, Lord, they're all calling to complain," I imagined.

As the next song set started, the cohosts turned on the speakerphone and answered the first call. I put my hands over my ears, expecting to hear someone say, "I don't appreciate hearing about this when I haven't had time to digest my Wheaties." Instead, to my surprise, the caller was saying "thank you"!

The caller explained he had intestinal problems and had always wondered what to do in those situations. He was sincere in his appreciation. The next caller, and the next, and the next also said "thank you."

Questions born out of embarrassing situations and painful memories poured in. No one complained. The hour flew by. Later, as I thought about the calls, I realized my fear had been silly. People want to know how to handle bathroom and bodily noise etiquette. These natural occurrences are part of our lives. The average adult produces one to eight cups of gas per day (depending on your food intake and various health factors). This creates the need to burp an average of 15 times daily.[1] In other words, for all of us, sometimes a bit of air is going to slip out one way or the other.

We're basically held hostage to our bodily noises. Although we can consciously control our words, thoughts, impulses, attitudes, actions, and beliefs, we find that our intestinal tracts... well, they're going to do what they're going to do without asking permission. When this happens, our dignity is left paralyzed with doubt about the right course of action to recover from our body's betrayal. The poor souls around us are equally embarrassed and perplexed about how to respond.

The calls that day didn't come from giggling 11-year-olds. They came from men and women who wanted to know how to handle with decorum their coughing fits, loud bathroom noises, burps, runny noses, gas bubbles, and all the rest. Their responses inspired me to include this kind of etiquette in my classes and seminars for both adults and children.

As you present these manners to your children or teens, prepare yourself for giggles or even laughing fits. I've taught these skills to thousands of children, and I deal with them with my own two boys. Reactions happen with every lesson. That's fine because they're laughing and learning at the same time.

With these practical lessons, you're giving your children a foundation of knowledge that will serve them well as they mature. Right now they might think passing gas is funny. However, one day they will feel mortified when they accidently let out a ten-decibel toot. And when that day comes, you will have prepared them to handle the situation with as little embarrassment as possible. That's an excellent gift to give!

In addition to imparting skills for handling unexpected sounds, the skills that follow explain good manners while in the bathroom, polite ways for children to ask to use the bathroom, and the best way to take care of a runny nose or cough while in public.

Bathroom Behavior

There's nothing like being greeted by "gifts" left by someone who used the toilet before you. Children are eager to leave the restroom quickly after they potty, so flushing needs to be stressed until you're certain it's a habit for them. Teach them to flush and stay in the bathroom (or stall if in a public restroom) until they see the toilet bowl empty and start to refill with fresh water.

When using a public bathroom, give a "friendly flush" as you're using the toilet. Letting others hear the sound of flushing, even a couple of times, is more courteous than forcing them to hear the sounds of nature coming from your stall.

Using friendly flushes is also a good idea when you're a guest in someone's home and using a bathroom that is next to a room where other guests are being entertained. For example, many half bathrooms are located right off the dining room, living room, or family room, where other guests might be able to hear bathroom noises.

If you need to vomit in a public restroom, use friendly flushes as well.

Of course, be sensitive to water shortages. Flush only once if there are water restrictions.

ℳom to ℳom

Have you ever tried to wash your hands in a public restroom and found the sink, countertop, and even the floor near the sink so wet you didn't have a place to set your purse? Me too! As a result, we end up holding our handbags with our knees and bending over the sink from as far away as possible to keep our clothes dry. Washing and drying our hands shouldn't be such a struggle! This all happens because people fail to follow simple and thoughtful etiquette. After washing and drying your hands, use your paper towel to clean up any water left behind on the sink.

When I'm drying a sink, many times I'll notice the ladies next to me watch me for a moment. I know what they're thinking: "That's a good idea. I never thought of it before." Then they take their paper towels and start wiping their sinks too!

Asking to Visit the Restroom

When visiting someone else's home, the same good manners apply. All the child needs to say is, "May I please be excused for a moment?" He doesn't need to specifically ask permission to use the bathroom. After all, what host is going to say, "No, we don't allow guests to use our bathrooms"?

What should your children do if they don't know where the bathroom is located or which one they should use? They simply need to excuse themselves and ask where to go. For example, "Excuse me, please. I'll be back in a moment. Which way to the restroom, Mrs. Keaton?"

Asking to Be Excused from the Table

By the time a child is in the third grade, she is old enough to be taught that it's best not to mention the bathroom at the table. Practice this at home during meals. Instead of announcing, "I'm going to the bathroom. I'll be back in a minute," your children can be taught to say, "May I please be excused for a minute?"

Younger children should ask permission to be excused from the table, but if tweens and teens are mature enough, they can simply say, "Please excuse me. I'll be right back."

When children learn how to excuse themselves from the table without stating a reason, they may test their limits. You'll need to make it clear that the only reasons they can be excused from the table during a meal are to use the restroom, cough, blow their nose, and such. Asking to be excused and saying they'll be back in a minute is not appropriate if they simply want to text their best friend or check in on Facebook.

Burps

When it comes to bodily noises, let's start with the lesser of the evils, and work our way up. (Or would that be down?)

When You Feel a Burp Coming On

1. Keep your lips closed and try to be as quiet as possible.

2. Take your left hand (your right hand if you're left-handed) and make a fist. Raise your fist to your mouth and burp into the part where your thumb and first (pointer) finger meet one another.

3. Turn your head to one shoulder as you silently burp into your fist. Which side to turn your head? Well, if there's no one on one side, choose that side. If there's someone on both sides, you've got a choice to make. Who will mind the least? If your neighbor is on your right, and your sister is on your left, turn your head to your left. It's no disrespect, it just goes with being family!

4. Say "Pardon me" to no one in particular but so that anyone who heard you burp will also hear your confession.

If You're Near Someone Who Burps

The less said, the better. If he apologizes or looks embarrassed, don't say anything, but simply smile a little smile that says, "Been there, done that!" Do this well, and you're going to be a hero!

If the person says "excuse me" and you feel you must respond (really, though, you don't have to say anything), a simple "of course" or "certainly" is all that's needed.

Passing Gas

I don't even like typing the words *passing gas*, let alone experiencing them. This is the bodily function people dread happening to them or anyone near them. Here's how to handle "air" with delicacy and discretion.

If You Pass Gas

Passing gas is called a *social unmentionable*. That means that regardless of what sound occurs, shhh! We don't need to talk about it!

There is a possible exception to the rule of silence. If you're with family or just a few dear friends and you pass gas and feel you must say something, then simply say "excuse me." But, really, you don't have to say a word! (Doesn't that make you feel better?)

When in a crowd or with strangers, usually you'll never mention that anything happened. "Owning it" is not actually the best choice. Because it's a social unmentionable, it's best not to draw attention to it.

If You're with Someone Who Passes Gas

If the person who passes the gas says "excuse me," simply give a little smile and be quick to carry on the conversation you were having prior to the incident.

Passing gas is embarrassing for the offender and the offended. Encourage your child to resist the urge to say anything or to laugh at the expense of the other person.

If a smell becomes too much for you, simply say "excuse me," and leave the room without explanation. When you return, no explanation is needed either. (You'll rarely need to take this action.)

Sniffles, Sneezes, Coughs, and More

Here are some how-to's for handling sniffles, sneezes, coughs, and other everyday occurrences.

Covering Sneezes and Coughs

Whenever you have congestion or a cough, carry a supply of tissues with you. When you cough or sneeze, cover your mouth and nose with a tissue.

Hold your tissue with your nondominant hand. If you're left-handed, keep the tissue in your right hand and vice versa. That way, when you hand someone an item, you won't be using the hand that held the tissue. This simple step effectively slows down the spread of germs.

Carry a zip-top baggie so you can dispose of tissues after use. When you get home, you can sanitarily throw away the day's tissues without anyone accidently touching one.

Use tissues instead of Grandma's dainty and lovely hanky. A hanky will retain all the germs, and each time you go to retrieve it, your hands are reexposed.

If you don't have a tissue in hand, you need to take other steps to prevent the spread of germs. Many of us have been taught to cover our noses and mouths with

> ### Mom to Mom
>
> You might want to establish a rule with your children that they apologize at home for releasing air around family members with a simple, "Excuse me, please." Otherwise, you're likely to be playing a lot of giggle-filled games of "I didn't do it; he did!"
>
> In public, as long as your child wasn't doing it on purpose, passing gas is just as embarrassing for him as it is for grown-ups. It's kind to allow children to follow the adult-level protocol of keeping it a social unmentionable. If your child has a gassy moment, don't announce loudly, "Christopher, say 'excuse me'!"

our hands when we cough or sneeze, but that's just about the worst advice we could follow. Afterward, our hands are full of germs that we transfer to everything we touch. Here are two better ways to handle the situation.

Bend your arm and cough into the inner part of your elbow. The downside of this method is that unless you're super limber, you'll never get your nose and mouth close enough to your elbow to catch all the germs. In addition, the germs are now all over your arm. If you accidently bump into anyone or anything, the germs are spread.

Even better, cough into your shoulder. Why? You're less likely to rub shoulders than to rub elbows with someone else. This will help keep the germs on you and prevent the droplets from being carried through the air to others. This is a great one for all of us to remember and to teach our children.

What to Say After Sneezes and Coughs

After you sneeze or cough, quietly say, "Excuse me." Your apology is offered to no one in particular but to everyone in your general vicinity, friend and stranger alike. If someone says "bless you" or "God bless you," respond by saying "thank you."

You never know about sneezes. Sometimes there's just one, sometimes they come in twos or threes, and sometimes we have sneezing fits. Because of this, slowly and silently count to three after someone sneezes before you speak. In the three seconds it takes you to do so, the other person will have time to sneeze again if she's going to. Usually, one time of saying "God bless you" is enough. More than that can distract from what's going on in the room—the class, church service, meeting, movie, or whatever it might be.

If you find yourself in the midst of a coughing or sneezing fit, excuse yourself from those around you and go to a private area. When you return, simply say, "Excuse me."

Dining with a Cold

Here are some special considerations for dining with others when you have a cold, cough, or allergies.

- If you need to cough or sneeze and you're caught without a tissue at the dining table, you may cover your mouth and nose with your napkin. Then ask for a new napkin.

- However, never use your napkin to wipe your nose. If you have a tissue at the table, you may use it to wipe (not blow) your nose.

- Never blow your nose in front of others. The noise is very irritating to some, especially while eating!

- If you don't have a tissue, it's fine to ask those around you if they have one.

Show Me, Please!

Here's a way to extend your children's or teens' grasp of the skills of this chapter. It will help them not only remember the skills but also develop muscle memory of what to do when they sneeze, cough, blow their nose, or burp. The game is just like Simon says, but it's called "Show me, please." Hand your child a tissue and explain, "I will tell you some things to do, but you should only do them when I say 'Show me, please' first." Then give several instructions, one at a time, for body noise etiquette concerning the best ways to sneeze, cough, blow noses, or burp. Sometimes say "Show me, please," and sometimes leave out the word *please*. Gradually speed up the instructions. This game will begin to build muscle memory, which will eventually make your child's reactions automatic. Oh yes, and prepare for a lot of giggling.

"Show me, please, what to say if you burp."

"Show me, please, what to say if someone you're with burps."

"Show me, please, what to do if you cough."

"Show me, please, what to do if you sneeze."

"Show me, please, what to say if you make a gassy sound."

"Show me, please, what to say if someone you're with makes a gassy sound."

"Show me, please, what to do if you have to blow your nose."

"Show me, please, what to do if you sneeze."

"Show me, please, what to do if you have to blow your nose at the table."

Etiquette and the Laws of Physics

I don't often—okay, I never—quote physics or engineering principles, but I'm about to do it now. There is a law of physics that rings true for personal interactions, and here it is: For every action there is an equal and opposite reaction (Newton's third law of motion). In other words, every action or word we speak has an effect on others that elicits a response.

For our tenth wedding anniversary, Kent and I planned a rare night on the town. I looked forward to our romantic interlude for weeks. I had a manicure and pedicure, bought a new little black dress and high heels, had my hair done, and even lost three pounds just for the occasion. We were seated at a beautiful table at our town's most highly regarded restaurant.

The man at the table next to us looked to be in his early sixties and was very animated. He seemed perfectly capable of leaving the table if he had wanted. Instead, he loudly honked, blew, coughed, and snorted mucus throughout his meal. Our looks and the looks of others from nearby tables didn't discourage him from continuing to launch nasal assaults.

Both Kent and I lost our appetites. It was a Saturday night, and the restaurant was packed. We asked for another table, but there wasn't one. It's a running joke between us now. But that night, one man's lack of bodily manners exterminated the enchantment of our romantic dinner with sounds as obnoxious as a bug zapper killing pests at a summer picnic.

We teach our children bathroom and bodily noise etiquette so they realize the impact their natural actions can have on those near them. This way they can be proactive in helping to keep the negative reactions of others to their snorts, burps, and worse from embarrassing them. I think even Mr. Newton would approve!

Inspiration and Application

1. Jesus said, "Let your light so shine before men that they may see your moral excellence and your praiseworthy, noble, and good deeds and recognize and honor and praise and glorify your Father Who is in heaven" (Matthew 5:16 AMP). How does taking

a moment to wipe up splashed water around the sink help you showcase Christ's care for all people?

2. Sneezing is mentioned only once in the Bible. It's found in 2 Kings 4:35, when God uses Elisha to raise the Shunammite's son back to life. "Elisha turned away and walked back and forth in the room and then got on the bed and stretched out on him once more. The boy sneezed seven times and opened his eyes" (NIV). Elisha showed such personal care in the way he sought God to raise the boy from the dead. We must also show personal care if we want to accurately express Christ's care to others. Why do you think the Bible mentions the fact that the boy sneezed and even tells us how many times he did so?

3. What are your polite options if a person with you burps?

4. If someone says "bless you" or "God bless you" after you sneeze, what should you say to her in return, and why is it important to say it?

5. List three tips you learned from this chapter that you'll apply in your everyday encounters and pass along to your children.

14

Life Skills Learned at the Dining Table

I had a friend whose family had dinner together every day. The mother would tuck you in at night and make breakfast in the morning. It just seemed so amazing to me.

MOON UNIT ZAPPA

Etiquette IQ Quiz

1. When setting the table, place and salad forks are properly laid...

    A. to the left of the plate

    B. to the right of the plate

    C. on top of the folded napkin

2. A place spoon is _____ part of your dinner place setting.

    A. always

    B. sometimes

    C. never

3. Tradition teaches us that when setting the table and eating, the cutting edge of your knife should...

    A. face you

    B. face away from you

    C. face you when setting the table and face away from you when laid on your plate in between bites*

---

*Answers: 1) A 2) B 3) A.

Our most meaningful and memorable life events are celebrated with food. Even before we were born, many of us had a baby shower, where people gathered around food to share gifts and conversation in anticipation of our arrival. Thus began the cycle.

Soon after your birth, there was probably a christening or baptism or dedication ceremony, which was normally followed by brunch or lunch. Then came your first birthday. The cake was as much a centerpiece of the day as you were. The years that followed brought childhood birthday parties, and you were probably as excited about the menu (pizza, hot dogs, chicken nuggets, and other childhood favorites) as you were about the party games and gifts.

Holidays brought with them the excitement of seeing grandparents, cousins, aunts, and uncles. Your family communed around the table, sharing the Easter ham, Thanksgiving turkey, and Christmas roast. The table experience contributed to your fond holiday memories as much as the gifts you received or other holiday traditions.

One day, too soon for your parents' liking but perhaps not soon enough for yours, you were the guest of honor at your high school graduation party. The "Congratulations, Graduate" banner hung on the wall near the finger foods and sodas. Within a few years you celebrated your college graduation, first job, and promotions over meals.

When you became a member of the workforce, the days started moving at a quicker pace. On one of them, a certain someone asked you out to dinner. That night, time seemed to do the impossible.

It stopped.

You realized you had just talked to each other for five hours straight. You laughed together about how it seemed as if only an hour or so passed.

Then one day that someone took you to a special dinner and asked if you'd do him the honor of becoming his wife.

Your "Yes!" brought a slew of "I do" events. An engagement party, a shower, a bridal lunch, your rehearsal dinner, a wedding reception...all celebrated by dining.

The excitement of your newlywed days passed into a year or more of happily wedded routine. An anniversary dinner or two later and you were able to share the blessed news that your first child was on his or her way.

Several months later, you were again the guest of honor at a baby shower. But this time, you were the mom-to-be. With that new life inside of you, a new cycle of sharing life's milestones around the table begins.

Preparing Children for Adult Life

As each child is born, you add an extra place at your dining table as happily as you do in your heart. That's good because the everyday meals around the family table have the biggest impact on who our children will become. Their values, their self-perception, and their way of interacting with the world will be caught and taught during conversations around the table.

At the dining table, the small victories (your oldest won her weekly swimming meet) and the little heartaches (your youngest child's goldfish died) are given the attention they deserve. As the events of each day are shared over casserole and rolls, tummies are filled, love is shown, and your family identity is planted. Your conversations nourish your children's growing character as much as the vegetables nourish their growing bodies.

Families need to dine together three or more times a week, sharing food and conversation (but not TV and electronics), if children are to have strong values and feel secure, loved, accepted, and happy. Research proves it. These studies reinforce the importance of gathering our families around the table. Here are three examples.

In 1996 Dr. Catherine Snow, professor of education at Harvard's Graduate School of Education, completed an eight-year study of 65 families. Her findings determined that "dinnertime was of more value to child development than playtime, school, and story time."[1]

"Dr. Blake Bowden of Cincinnati Children's Hospital Center studied 527 teenagers to determine what family and lifestyle characteristics were related to good mental health and adjustment. Dr. Bowden and his colleagues found that kids who ate dinner with families at least five times per week (at home or in a restaurant) were the least likely to take drugs, feel depressed, or get into trouble with the law. The more poorly adjusted teens, in contrast, ate with their parents an average of three or fewer evenings a week."

"A survey conducted by the University of Chicago revealed that a majority of graduate students, when asked where they got most of their ideas about morality and religion, responded, 'Through conversation with the family at meal times.'"

Unfortunately, our children are sometimes scheduled to be more places each week than a commercial airline pilot. Tightly packed afternoons and evenings of soccer, dance, karate, baseball, cheerleading, hockey, gymnastics, and the like result in children who grow up to be good kickers, dancers, and goalies. But these activities don't equip our children with the interpersonal skills they need to enter adulthood fully prepared for the discussions, decisions, and demands of adult life.

When we decide that sending our children and teens to extracurricular activities most evenings is more important than having them with us at dinner, we undervalue our impact on them. In fact, studies indicate that teens actually want to spend more time with their parents, not less, as they get older. But the popular culture tries to contradict this truth.

The table is the best place for our children to learn about the ebb and flow of conversations, listening, politely disagreeing, asking before taking, and gratitude for food and the people who provide and prepare it. Here is the place to share our family heritage of recipes and history, our views on politics, and our reasons for believing what we believe about God and His grace. At the table we share with one another our family's agendas, learn to wait for others to finish, help one another to clean up, and so much more.

The most impacting, profound, gentle, and caring teacher of all is our own example, demonstrated over the unhurried pace of years of family dinners.

But Does Form Matter?

I had flown overnight to Memphis to conduct an etiquette dinner for a team of executives. These 20 or so men and women ranged from their thirties to sixties. They each earned six figures or more a year and traveled extensively representing their company. I was sent to make sure they knew everything there was to know about dining so they could represent their company well and concentrate on making deals over dinner instead of wondering which bread plate was theirs. They weren't at this dinner by choice. Their divisional vice president had made it mandatory.

It was seven in the evening. The executives had been in meetings since seven that morning. When I met them, they were exhausted and hungry. I overheard one of the men as he entered the room say to another, "I've been eating for forty-seven years. I don't drool or fart at the table. I can't believe I have to be at this [expletive] dinner. My mom taught me how to eat. This lady can't teach me anything I don't know."

About 40 minutes into our two-hour dinner, the same gentleman raised his hand to ask, "Maralee, you don't make your kids follow all these rules at home, do you? If so, they must hate you. You're sharing so much, and I haven't heard most of it before. You can't tell me you know anyone else who knows or does all this stuff."

This 47-year-old man was overwhelmed to discover how much he never knew that he never knew.

I remained silent for a moment, thinking about what I should say. Then I bent down and slowly removed both of my four-inch high-heel pumps. The group grew quiet as they watched me. In my bare feet and power suit I leaned against the lectern in our private dining room and said this to the group.

> A lot of very smart people know everything I'm sharing with you tonight and more. I can assure you, my boys don't hate me. In my house we eat dinner at the kitchen table. Shoes [I held up mine] are optional. The napkins are paper. The plates are from JCPenney. The conversation is fun. The love is abundant. The food is Southern. If you eat all your vegetables, you get dessert. I make an awesome blueberry cobbler!
>
> I introduce the dining rules one at a time. They're a source of confidence for my boys—not drudgery. This isn't about pretense. This is about purposefulness. My boys are prepared to

eat beef Wellington at the White House or wings at a Super
Bowl party. The rules aren't limiting; they're freeing. They free
us from doubt, from being ill-prepared, and from looking as if
we haven't been anywhere in the world except down our own
street. These are pretty good traits in boys. I can't wait to see
how well these skills serve them as men.

Everyone in the room applauded—loudly. The executive who asked
the question responded, "Now, especially since you make blueberry cob-
bler, I wish you were my wife!" We laughed together. (I waited awhile
before putting my shoes back on. They were killing my feet!)

What my executive client didn't realize at that moment was that once
the dining skills are learned, they are easy to use. After all, doing something
the right way—whether mastering a Pilates stretch, getting a yoga position
just so, or handling our knife and fork in the way tradition and uncom-
monly good sense teach us to—is usually as easy as doing these things the
wrong way. Someone simply needs to show us how.

Does the form we use at the table offer us any benefit? Is proper form
worth following? Is it worth the time and energy we spend to teach our
children these things? Absolutely! Christ knew and followed the social
forms of His day. As His ambassadors, we should do the same.

A Note Before We Jump In

Many etiquette books deal exclusively with dining skills. Some are
200 pages or longer. The following chapters on dining skills aren't meant to
teach every skill and every exception to the rules.

Instead, I've included the things I'm teaching and reinforcing with my
own two boys. These guidelines give our children a breadth of knowledge that
will serve them well now and as adults. Due to space limitations I'm not able
to list the *why* for each skill. I will say in general that some skills have come
down through history and have remained unchanged for hundreds of years
because they still make sense today (and they pay homage to our past). Other
skills have changed to keep up with our modern sensibilities.

For example, nowadays you're much more likely to find a saltshaker on the table than individual saltcellars with tiny salt spoons at each place setting. Saltshakers make more sense because they can be shared by everyone at the table, which means you only have to buy one. That's why saltcellars, asparagus tongs, and grape knives are not in this book. Here you'll discover how to prepare your children for their everyday encounters.

Years of experience with many students have shown me that children and teens actually enjoy learning (and using) dining skills because these behaviors are tactile, concrete, and measurable. I always suggest that parents teach dining skills early because the learning process is a positive experience. Children and teens enjoy receiving the immediate compliments you and others can give them on their great table manners. After all, there are never more than a few hours between now and the next meal. However, weeks could pass before they meet a new person and receive positive feedback on the way they introduce themselves or others, and the next birthday party invitation may not arrive for months. Dining manners allow children to show you they shine today!

Setting the Table

Before we get into general manners for the table and the how-to's of eating certain foods, let's look at how to set the table.

Knowing which side of the plate your glass and your bread plate are placed saves you from uncertainty at every banquet, fund-raiser, and formal event you attend. When you sit down at a table for eight, everything on the table is so crowded together, it's easy to wonder, "Is this my glass or the next person's?" This isn't a question you really want to ask if the person next to you is a stranger!

This confusion happens a lot. People who have recognized me at banquets have come over to where I'm sitting and whispered, "Excuse me, Maralee. Is my bread plate on my right or my left?"

Once at a five-course meal my husband was attending for work, everyone was commenting about how they had never seen so many forks and glasses on a table at one time. Then somebody said, "Hey, I bet Kent knows.

His wife is the Manners Mentor on TV and radio." Long story short, Kent ended up leading an etiquette lesson for the people at his table and the tables nearest him as he patiently answered one question after another. He was beaming when he walked in the kitchen door that night. "Hon!" he exclaimed. "At dinner tonight everyone asked me questions about the etiquette of their place settings. I was able to answer every question and throw in a few pointers too."

Knowing the blueprint of the place settings is a source of confidence that children and teens can learn now and benefit from throughout life.

The Family Place Setting

We'll look at two types of table settings. The first is a simple, everyday table setting. It's a great way to set the table each evening, and I call it the family place setting. You can teach about the family place setting using three simple steps.

Family place setting.

1. Place the plate

We set the plate first because we'll be placing items to its right and left. In the family place setting, three items go to the right of the plate and three to the left. (These equal numbers on either side of the plate make it easier for children to remember!)

2. Place Items with Five Letters to the Right

To help our children (and us!) remember which three items are placed to the right of the plate, remember that they are all five-letter words, just like the word *right*.

Knife. Place the knife next to the plate with the cutting edge facing the plate. Hundreds of years ago, the table knife was also used to slaughter the animals. Since that time, it has been considered bad form to allow the cutting edge of the knife to face anyone else at the table.

Glass. The glass goes above the point of the knife. If you'll be using more than one glass, such as one for water and one for iced tea, the water glass goes above the point of the knife, and any other glasses go to the right of the water glass.

Spoon. The spoon is placed to the right of the knife. There's no need to place spoons on the table if you know they're not going to be used. For most family dinners, a spoon isn't required. Once a child has the manual dexterity to use a fork, all vegetables and starches (rice, corn, mashed potatoes, and such) are correctly eaten with a fork. A spoon would be correct for gelatin, applesauce, soup, and such.

3. Place Items with Four Letters to the Left

The word *left* has four letters, and so do the names of the three items placed on the table to the left of your plate. (We have to tweak the words a little bit to get four letters, but the memory aid helps.)

Fork. The fork is placed to the left of the plate but not on top of the napkin. That's because after we sit down, one of the first things we do is place the napkin on our lap. We can't put a napkin on our lap if the fork is on top of it without touching the fork. After you touch a piece of silverware, it's not to be placed back on the table.

Wipe (the napkin). The closed (or folded) edge of the napkin faces the plate. When the fold is placed this way, it is easier for us to correctly open the napkin after it's on our lap.

Roll (bread plate). The bread plate is placed above the fork. Bread plates aren't necessary for family dinners. Placing your roll or bread on the side of your dinner plate is fine. However, teach your children about bread plates

Mom to Mom

Your children can have fun as they practice setting the table. Get a one-gallon resealable bag for each child and fill it with a dinner-size paper plate, sandwich-size paper plate (for use as a bread plate), paper or plastic cup, paper napkin, and plastic knife, fork, and spoon. Use colorful plates or have your children decorate plain ones.

Teach your children the three items that go on each side of the plate. When they have mastered the family place setting, they'll be proud to show everyone their new skill by setting the family table.

because they're common at many family restaurants and at all fine restaurants and formal meals. Restaurants often serve bread before the first course, and servers bring bread plates so you have a place to lay your bread. In this case, you can place your bread plate directly in front of you and then move the bread plate to the left of your dinner plate when the first course is brought to the table. Bread plates also keep bread from getting soggy from gravy, sauces, or juices on our plate.

A Formal Place Setting

Formal place settings vary depending on the number of courses and the food being served. Here you'll see a formal place setting set for a four-course meal. Let's see what is on the menu and then change our family place setting to make it suitable for the anniversary dinner we're hosting for our best friend and her husband and children.

Lobster Bisque

• • •

Spring Greens and Goat Cheese Salad
Raspberry Dressing
Orange Marmalade Chicken
Brown and Wild Rice
Steamed Asparagus

• • •

Apple Tartlets with Vanilla Hazelnut Creme Anglaise

Fairly formal place setting.

Let's look at what has been added to the family place setting and why.

Additions to the Right

Soupspoon. This replaces the regular place spoon.

Second glass. This has been added for iced tea or any other beverage. Its proper place is to the right of our water glass. If you have a long-handled iced beverage spoon for sugar to be stirred into tea, place it on the outside of the place setting, to the right of the soupspoon.

Additions to the Left

Salad fork. This is placed to the left of the place fork. Utensils are arranged in a place setting so that we use the one farthest from the plate first and move in toward our plate for each consecutive course. In formal meals, the salad is sometimes served after the entrée so that guests won't fill up on lettuce before they enjoy the delicious main dish. For these meals, the salad fork is placed to the right of the place fork.

Butter spreader. Traditionally this is laid across the top of the bread plate with the spreading edge facing you. A more modern approach (and the one I use) is to lay the butter spreader on the right side of the bread plate, as it is shown in the illustration. This prevents us from having to reach over the plate to pick up the spreader and keeps us from getting butter on our long-sleeve shirts and blouses.

Mom to Mom

Place cards can be used for a romantic dinner for two and should be used anytime you have a meal with six or more guests. It's time consuming to tell that many people where to sit, so making up place cards in advance is preferable. You may wonder, why not just invite people to sit wherever they like? Hosts are responsible to provide for the comfort of their guests. Guests are most comfortable sitting next to people they have something in common with. You know each of your guests, so your forethought on who would make a good tablemate for whom is a precious gift to them.

If not everyone at the table knows one another, it's nice to write each person's name on both sides of their place cards. This way, guests can read each other's names.

Married couples are usually seated apart. They have a lifetime to talk to each other. They can compare notes during the car ride home!

Additions Above the Plate

Dessertspoon and dessert fork. The fork rests closest to the dinner plate, and the tines point to the right. The spoon sits above the fork, and the bowl of the spoon points toward the left.

Many years ago an eight-year-old girl in one of my Manners Mentor classes suggested this visual aid to remember which direction to use for the dessertspoon and dessert fork. Pretend they are sunflowers. The dessert fork is planted next to the other forks but grows up over the plate and tilts toward the glass. The dessertspoon is planted with the other spoons but grows up over the plate and the dessert fork and tilts toward the bread plate. I've never had a student (youth or adult) not remember how to set her dessert service after hearing this explanation!

Place card. This is set directly above the dessert spoon and fork. It shows us that a special place has been prepared in advance for us.

We Come Full Circle Around the Table

The table experience shapes our tradition, our outlook on life, and even our character. We gather around the table with friends and family to nourish our bodies and souls. The cycle of everyday meals and of celebrating life's milestones begins even before we are born and continues throughout life. Then one day, after we're gone, those who love us and are left behind will come together in the hours after our funeral to mourn, remember, comfort one another, and celebrate the life we lived. They'll gather around the table over shared tears...and food.

Inspiration and Application

1. What are three benefits our children and teens receive from sharing in family dinners without TV and electronics? How many times at a minimum each week do studies show families should eat together?

2. When setting a family place setting, how many items go on the right and left of the dinner plate? List each of the items, making sure that the items on the left are each spelled with four letters and the items on the right are each spelled with five letters.

3. How do place cards benefit your guests?

4. In the fairly formal place setting, we added a dessertspoon and dessert fork above the dinner plate. Which directions do the bowl of the spoon and the tines of the fork point? What example was given that can help us remember how to set the dessert service?

15

FUNdamentals of Dining and Secret Signals

The world was my oyster, but then I used the wrong fork.
RALPH WALDO EMERSON

Etiquette IQ Quiz

1. From which direction should you approach your dining table chair in order to sit down?

   A. from the left of the chair

   B. from the right of the chair

   C. Either direction is correct when sitting down. When exiting the chair, it's considered correct to exit from your left.

2. When you leave the table while dining, where do you place your napkin to signal that you've only left for a minute or so and will be returning to continue eating?

   A. on the table to the left of your plate

   B. on the table to the right of your plate

   C. on your chair

3. Picturing your plate as a clock. What time should the tines of the fork point to when you lay it on your plate in-between bites?

   A. ten

   B. twelve

   C. two*

Answers: 1) B 2) C 3) A*.

Anytime I have the honor of sharing etiquette skills, I am happy. However, of everything I teach, nothing makes me happier than sharing dining skills. I suppose it has to do with my experience of meeting Kent's mom for the first time over dinner. Because I was confident in my dining skills, I was the calm, at ease, poised lady I had prayed to become since I was eight. That was when I realized who I was in God's eyes.

I pray you'll feel my excitement and join with me in mastering these skills and sharing them with your children. Let me encourage you not to let the busyness of life keep you from using these skills every day. Our children deserve the benefits that result when they make a habit of using them. That will happen only with daily use.

In the previous chapter we learned the how and why of setting each place at the table. Now let's see how to use each of the items in our place setting. With dining etiquette, there's pretty much one established way to do something, and learning that one skill for each scenario is simple, straightforward, and fun! From first bite to last, the mechanics of dining are the same whether we're seven, thirty-seven, or seventy-seven. Learn the how-to once, practice it until it's automatic, and you're done!

Whether you are unfolding your napkin, holding your knife and fork correctly, or using the special rest and finished signals, you'll enjoy a lovely rhythm as everyone at the table uses the same dining skills. Like dancers on a stage, you will experience the beauty of moving in unison.

A Note Before We Begin

There are two styles of dining: the continental style and the zigzag style (also called the American style). Both styles are correct. For the purpose of this book, I'm sharing the zigzag style because it's most commonly used in the United States (although the continental style is used by most of the rest of the world). I don't like to teach children or teens both styles until they have mastered one. I've found that too often they get confused and begin to incorporate parts of each style, creating a combination that isn't a correct version of either one.

Secret Signals and Other Fundamental Dining Skills

Some lovely traditional nonverbal signals tell servers and our fellow diners all sorts of things about our intentions while dining. Are we full? Do we plan to eat more? Are we leaving the table for a moment? Or are we finished eating and not planning to return to the table? These are all signaled by what we do with our napkin, knife, and fork.

Many people don't know these signals, but knowing them helps us to avoid sending mixed messages. They communicate our intentions so we don't have to waste valuable conversation by asking, "Are you going to eat the rest of that?" and other questions.

I call them *secret signals*. I share with the children in my Manners Mentor classes that many boats carry flags to send messages to everyone who knows how to read them. When dining, we send signals with our napkin, knife, and fork.

Each one of these items has two signals—the rest signal and the finished signal. Three items (napkin, knife, and fork) with two signals each (resting and finished) equal six secret signals. They're so fun and easy to learn and use that even children as young as five or six years old can master them in a few weeks.

We need to attend to other dining skills as well, so let's begin with the first thing we do when we come to the table—sit down.

Coming to the Table

Dining etiquette can seem arbitrary until we know the reason why a particular skill has lasted through the centuries and still applies today.

It's easy to think, "Why in the world does it matter whether I approach my chair from the left or the right?" Here's the answer: The established direction (from the right) lets those who are already sitting know what to expect so they can help by moving a bit to give you the room you need to enter or exit your chair. (You exit the chair from the same direction you entered it.) In addition, if several people are sitting down or leaving the table at the same time, this keeps them from bumping into each other.

Taking Your Seat

Remain standing. The hostess should be the first to sit unless she says to everyone, "Please sit. I'll join you in a moment." Three steps will get you in your seat with minimum fuss:

- Stand directly behind the chair and use both hands to pull it out from the table.

- Step to the right of the chair so that you will move to your left as you sit.

- Sit down while pulling the chair to the table.

This can be confusing for many children. It confuses me! So here's another way to remember. When I'm standing next to the chair and about to sit down, my left leg is closest to the chair. I remember the feeling of my left leg touching the chair, and that makes it easy for me to remember which direction to enter and exit.

If you don't eat with it, put it away. Cell phones and all other electronics, books, and purses should not be placed on the table. Electronics are put away. Books and papers are placed under your chair. Your purse should be left either on your lap with the napkin covering it (if it's small) or on the floor directly in front of your feet. A purse doesn't hang from the back of the chair because someone could easily bump into it or steal it. A purse is not placed on the floor next to your chair because others will have to step over it in order to enter and exit their chair.

Growing in Graciousness
(Next-Level Skills)

Pulling Out a Chair for a Lady

A gentleman still pulls out a lady's chair for her on social occasions. Before your son begins dating, let him practice respecting (and impressing!) young ladies by pulling out the chair for you. A dad will also want to pull out the chair for his daughter so she will be prepared should a young gentleman pull her chair out for her on a date.

Even in the adult classes I teach, everyone has questions about how to do this correctly. There are four simple steps.

1. Gentlemen, look at the lady, smile, and say "May I?" or "Allow me" as you stand behind her chair.

2. Ladies, smile and say "Thank you" as you move to the right of the chair (putting it on your left).

3. Gentlemen, pull the chair out and allow the lady to begin sitting. Push the chair in only until it touches the back of her knees. Then let go of the chair.

4. Ladies, as soon as you feel the chair touch the back of your legs, you can finish sitting down while sliding the chair the rest of the way forward yourself toward the table. Smile and say "thank you" to the gentleman!

In the past, etiquette required gentlemen to stand each time a lady came to or left the table on social occasions. Ladies, if the gentlemen do stand, it is a nice gesture of respect. If you prefer not to have your comings and goings emphasized this way, you can say sincerely, "Thank you! I feel honored that you have stood up for me. But since we're going to enjoy this event together for a while, you are welcome to stay comfortable in your seat when I come and go from the table."

Table Posture

Most people sit farther from the table than is correct. Sitting too far back causes us to bend down to our food more than we need, and it hinders us from sitting up straight and tall. It also lends to putting our elbows on the table and increases the likelihood of food falling off our fork and onto our lap.

To see whether you're seated close enough to the table, once seated, hold your four fingers straight and together, and bend your thumb under your hand. Next, place the side of your hand to the side of the table with your little finger touching the table and your pointer finger closest to you.

The table checker.

Scoot your chair up to the table until your midsection is touching your pointer finger. You will probably end up much closer to the table than you normally sit. The same four-finger distance applies to our children. Using their built-in "table checker" will be fun if you have fun telling them about it and everyone at the table is using it together!

Posture Skills

Sit straight and tall. Sit tall with your back near the back of the chair, or sit forward a little in a deep chair, still keeping your back straight.

Feet flat on the floor. For children whose feet don't touch the floor, remind them not to swing their legs back and forth or to wrap their feet around the chair legs.

Four on the floor. Keep all four feet of the chair on the floor. Children and especially teen boys often want to lean back on the back two legs of the chair.

Don't cross your legs at the knees. It's hard for most of us not to want to cross our legs. At the table it's important so that we don't accidentally bump the table. We also tend to sit up straighter when our legs aren't crossed.

In between bites, our hands go on our lap. This not only is good posture but also helps your napkin stay on your lap. Rest both hands on your lap when not using them to eat or drink.

When to Start to the Meal

Both children and adults may hesitate at the start of a meal, wondering when it's okay to reach for the napkin or to taste the fresh-baked bread on the table. Here are some tips to help you know what to do.

Everything waits for grace. A prayer of blessing for the food can be said either while everyone is standing at their dining chairs or as soon as everyone is seated. If you are seated, don't touch anything at the table, pass food or condiments, take a sip of your beverage, or place your napkin on your lap until after grace is said.

Follow the lead of the hostess. As the meal continues, allow the host or hostess to do everything first as a sign of respect. She's the first one to remove her napkin to her lap

Mom to Mom

Elbows on the table? *Psst...* I won't tell if you won't. Modern manners have evolved for our casual culture, and now it's fine to have our forearms on the table anytime we don't have food in front of us (before the server brings it, in between courses, and after the meal while we're talking at the table). However, it's also still correct to keep both hands on our lap. I haven't shared this new tidbit of information about it being okay to put our arms on the table with my children. All on their own, they manage to put their arms on the table a lot. If I let them know it's okay sometimes, they'll do it all the time!

after grace, the first to begin each course, and the one to invite everyone to leave the table after the meal is complete.

Placing Your Napkin

A friend of mine with a Hungarian background went with her family to meet relatives in Budapest for the first time about 30 years ago. She enjoyed many rich, homemade meals of chicken paprikash, steaming dumplings, and apple strudel. One of the things that brought much laughter to the table involved the napkin at each place setting.

As soon as the Americans sat down to eat, they placed their napkins on their laps. To their surprise, within minutes, fresh napkins appeared next to their plates at the table. If these napkins were dispatched to join the napkins already on their laps, more napkins promptly materialized. The Americans eventually realized that in Hungary, the napkin stays on the table. And if it goes missing, another takes its place.

Around the world, napkins are handled in many ways. However, in the United States, the napkin is placed on your lap. Pick the napkin up from the table and place it on your lap still folded as it was on the table. Don't open it in midair. Then unfold your dinner napkin until it's folded only one time (in half). Place the fold against your waist.

Growing in Graciousness
(Next-Level Skills)

How to Unfold Various Napkins

Large, dinner-size napkins are kept folded in half on your lap. Smaller napkins for tea or lunch are opened fully. This applies whether the napkin is paper or fabric.

Most people tend to open their dinner napkin all the way for maximum coverage. However, when they wipe their fingers, their clothes are likely to get stains from the napkin on them. When using our table checker to sit close enough to the table, very little of our lap is exposed for food to drop on it, so maximum coverage area isn't an issue.

Using Your Napkin

Looney Tunes characters made us laugh as they tucked billowing white napkins into their collars and commenced eating a meal with soup splashing and crumbs flying. However, that's not how we want our children to use their napkins at the table. Here are some practical guidelines on when, why, and how to use your napkin.

Wipe your fingers often. Make especially sure to wipe them before reaching for or passing anything at the table.

Wipe your fingers with the napkin in your lap. Anytime something is on your fingers, wipe them by lifting up slightly a corner of the top fold of your napkin while the bottom layer is resting in your lap.

Wipe your lips before drinking. In addition to wiping our lips when we feel we have something on our chin, it's proper to wipe them each time before taking a drink. That way food stains or lipstick won't show up on the rim of our glass for all the guests at the table to see throughout the meal.

Napkin Secret Signals

Has this scenario ever happened to you? You're at a restaurant and you're not quite finished with your meal, but you have to leave the table for a moment. You wonder how to make sure the server doesn't take your plate while you're gone. The answer is to use a secret signal with your napkin. Your children will love learning these signals and trying them out the next time you eat at a restaurant.

The rest signal. If you leave the table for any reason, signal to everyone else at the table and your server that you plan on coming right back to finish what's on your plate. Place your napkin, still folded in half carefully, on the seat of the chair just as it was on your lap. Push the chair under the table. This way people aren't left looking at a dirty napkin on the table while they're eating. (To avoid staining the chair cushion, remember to place the clean side of the napkin against the cushion.)

The finished signal. To signal the end of the meal, the host or hostess will be the first to remove her napkin from her lap and place it to the left of her plate (where she originally found it). Everyone else should then follow her lead. So that no one gets confused and mistakes a used napkin for a clean one, don't neatly refold a used napkin. Simply pick it up from the center and lay it loosely on the table as you get up to leave.

Silverware Savvy

Not all children have the manual dexterity to hold their utensils and cut their food in the way we're about to describe. That's fine. Show them the skills, review them from time to time, and use them yourself. They'll pick them up at their own time and pace.

My oldest mastered what I'm sharing with you here when he was seven. My nine-year-old still gets confused trying to hold his knife and fork properly. I have no doubt he'll get there...and long before his wedding day. I don't make it a point of frustration for him or for me. The importance of bonding and dining together are too important to allow table time to turn into a place of constant correction and frustration.

From time to time, I offer him a brief reminder lesson. One day I know he'll have his aha! moment. Then, just as when he was learning to swim, his wobbling efforts will morph into smooth mastery.

The Zigzag Style for Cutting Food

To cut a bite of food, follow these steps.

1. Hold your knife in your right hand and your fork in your left hand. Place your pointer fingers at the top of the handles, where the handle meets the blade of the knife or the tines of the fork. The hand you hold them in correlates to the side of the plate they're on in your place setting.

2. Press your fork into the food that needs to be cut, and position the knife in front of (above) the fork. Your fork stays closest to your body, making it easier to raise the food toward your mouth. Many children and teens will mistakenly place the knife in back of the fork or between the tines of the fork when trying to cut, making it awkward and hard for them.

3. Cut your food, don't saw it. Move the knife in one direction only (toward you). When cutting meat, you might have to make the same cut two or three times.

4. After cutting one bite, place your knife down on your plate in the resting signal position (the top right corner of the plate). Transfer (zigzag) your fork to your right hand and eat that one bite. While chewing or taking a drink, lay your fork on the plate instead of holding it in your hand in anticipation of your next bite.

5. For your next cut, return your fork to your left hand and pick up your knife with your right hand again. Repeat zigging and zagging throughout the meal!

Growing in Graciousness
(Next-Level Skills)

Once your children are old enough to cut their own food, teach them to cut only one bite at a time. This way, their food won't cool off too quickly, they won't eat too quickly, and their plate will look neater. (When they're little, though, it's fine to cut children's food all at once.)

Zigzag Just for Lefties

For my oldest son and the rest of the lefties in the world (about 15 percent of the population), each place setting is set in the standard way. However, everything about handling the utensils is reversed for the ease of the left-handed user. They will hold their knife in their left hand and fork in their right hand while cutting. They eat by zigzagging the fork to their left hand.

Secret Signals for Your Knife and Fork

You send silent signals with your silverware just as you do with your napkin. We've already learned the rest and finished signals for our napkin. Now it's time to discover where to lay your knife and fork on the plate between bites and when you've finished each course.

To help our children remember where to place their knife and fork, have them think of the plate as a clock.

The Rest Signal for Utensils

Lay your fork on your plate with the tines near the center of the plate and pointing to ten o'clock. The handle of your fork then naturally points to four o'clock.

Your knife lies above the fork across the top right-hand corner of your plate with the blade facing toward you. Leave a few inches of space between your knife and fork.

You'll have lots of opportunities during each meal to use the rest signal. A few of these times include taking a drink, talking to someone, eating a bite of bread or roll, passing food, using the salt and pepper, and anytime you leave the table but plan to return.

Growing in Graciousness
(Next-Level Skills)

Adjusting the Rest Position

If there is food on the plate at the four o'clock position, simply adjust the position of the fork. The time listed gives children an easy reference point, but common sense always rules. Make sure to tell this to younger children. I can say from experience that if you don't, you'll have little ones licking mashed potatoes off their fork handle at Christmas dinner proudly saying, "Look, Mommy! I signaled with my fork at ten o'clock, just like you taught me!"

The Finished Signal for Utensils

Signaling that you're finished is easy. In Manners Mentor classes I tell the students to think of the knife and fork as best friends and ask them, "Where do best friends want to always be? They always want to be side by..." The answer, of course, is they always want to be side by side. That's how we end each meal—with

the knife and fork together. Simply place your knife beside the fork on your plate at the ten o'clock position. Easy peasy!

The Comfort of Table Traditions

The commonality of everyone at the table sitting down, saying grace, placing our napkins on our laps, cutting our food, and signaling our intentions with our napkins, forks, and knives fosters community. The mechanics of learning these skills are easy and fun. Best of all, the form doesn't change with age. What you teach your child today will benefit him for a lifetime. Begin putting these skills into practice today, and your children will soon make a happy habit of using them in your home— an outpouring of your family's commitment to in-sync communion with one another around the table.

Mom to Mom

Using the finished signal is a thoughtful gesture toward the person clearing the table, especially when you add on this special tip. Leave the handles of your knife and fork extruding only about an inch off the plate. This allows for quieter and faster removal of the plates from the table. The person clearing can grasp the plate and the silverware with one hand without the silverware falling off the plate or clanging against it.

Mom to Mom

To help your child remember the rest and finished signals, gather two paper plates and two plastic knives and forks. Label one paper plate *rest* and the other *finished*. (If your child is old enough, have him write the words on the plates.) Use a brightly colored paper plate or a plain one that your child can decorate. With a low-temperature hot-glue gun, have your child adhere one knife and fork in the correct position on the rest plate, and the other knife and fork in the correct position on the finished plate. Children enjoy the activity. It's great practice, and the plates make wonderful reminders to place on the table until using the rest and finished signals becomes a habit.

Inspiration and Application

1. Paul urges us in 1 Corinthians 14:40, "Be courteous and considerate in everything." The same verse in the NIV reads, "Everything should be done in a fitting and orderly way." Paul was referring to being orderly in worship, but the same surely applies to everything we do. After all, creation shows us that God finds beauty in order. (Sunrise and sunset, high tide and low tide, the cycles of the moon each month, a time for planting and sowing, and the four seasons of the year are just a few examples of the order He built into our world.) God is also the source of the food on our plates. How can eating with attention to form (as opposed to simply gobbling food) and consideration for others around the table be a way to honor and worship Him?

2. Some people distort orderliness by taking it to an extreme. Our family table should be a place of joyful communion, encouragement, and laughter where relationships are nurtured and fond memories are formed. It should never resemble a military boot

camp dining hall. What are ways you can teach dining skills without shutting out the joyful, peaceful, and loving environment the dining table is meant to create for drawing our family together?

3. From which direction should you approach the dining table chair in order to sit down? From the chair's _____, which means moving to your _____. What are two benefits of everyone entering and exiting their dining chairs from the same direction?

4. Why is it better to have our dinner napkin folded in half when it's on our lap than to have it opened all the way?

5. Draw two plates in the spaces provided below. On the first plate, draw a knife and fork as you would lay them on your plate to signal that you're resting. On the second plate, draw a knife and fork laying on your plate to signal that you are finished eating.

Resting   Finished

16

Fast-Food to Five-Star Table Manners

*Strange to see how a good dinner
reconciles everybody.*
SAMUEL PEPYS

Etiquette IQ Quiz

1. Food should be passed around the table to your...

    A. right

    B. left

    C. To the right at the start of dinner. If someone is requesting seconds, then whichever direction is closest.

2. When someone asks for the pepper, you're correct to pass him or her...

    A. just the pepper, as requested

    B. both the salt and pepper

    C. Either *A* or *B* is correct.

3. Food is traditionally placed on your table by a server from your...
    A. left

    B. right

    C. Food is served from your left and drinks are served from your right.*

Answers: 1) C 2) B 3) A.*

The boys had the day off from school, so we decided to go out for lunch. In a rare unanimous vote, Marc and Corbett chose the same restaurant—our favorite little Thai place. The wind chimes tied to the inside of the front door tinkled our arrival and then clanked as the door swung shut. Recognizing us because we've eaten there so often, the grandmotherly owner smiled and welcomed us warmly. She picked up three menus and a coloring page and crayons for Corbett. With her heavy but quiet accent, she beamed at Corbett, hugging him with her words. "I remember your favorite color is orange, so I got you an orange crayon."

"Thank you very much," he replied, making a show of the strain in his voice as he slid the king-size chair out from the table.

"Oh, you're getting strong!" she complimented. Corbett was smitten by her attention. Standing next to Marc, she then spoke to him. "You're getting so tall! You're taller than me now. How old are you, again?"

He smiled proudly, sharing with her that he had just turned ten. "Ten? You're going to be a giant! You need to eat a big lunch so you keep growing! I'll bring a big, big portion."

"Do you want to order the usual or something different today?" she asked us. I smiled and looked at the boys, "The usual?" I asked them. They nodded their heads yes.

"It will be ready in a few minutes," our sweet hostess said. She patted Marc on the back and returned to put the unread menus back on the counter by the cash register, between the gold statue of Buddha in a pink unbuttoned shirt and a green glass bowl of tiny Tootsie Rolls.

The wind chimes tinkled and clanked again. A lady stepped into the tiny restaurant. Her shoulder-length blonde hair fell in loose curls against her back. She was close to six feet tall and model thin. From her designer handbag and shoes to her perfectly accessorized business dress, her outfit might have caused even a Beverly Hills fashionista a little case of envy.

The owner rang up her carryout order and offered her a seat while her food was being prepared. "Please sit anywhere. I'll bring you a salad with peanut dressing while you wait...no charge!" she said enthusiastically.

The beautiful lady, probably in her early thirties, sat down in one of the only empty tables—the one next to us.

"Is she famous?" Marc spoke softly to me, obviously noticing she was stunning.

"I don't recognize her," I quietly answered, although the thought had crossed my mind too.

We weren't the only ones who had noticed the beautiful lady. She seemed to have caught the eye of everyone in the small, crowded restaurant.

A waitress took only a minute to bring her the salad.

Corbett, overhearing our whispers, looked up from his coloring to see her. That's when this elegant visitor did the strangest thing I've ever seen anyone eating in public do.

She was alone at a table preset with silverware for four. Instead of unrolling one of the cloth napkins to take out a knife and fork, she picked up a handful of lettuce dripping with peanut dressing, leaned forward over the plate, and stuck the handful in her mouth, being careful not to let the dressing spill on her dress. While still chewing, she "daintily" licked the fingers of her right hand one by one before gathering her next handful of salad. She ate the two tomato wedges and the thick slice of cucumber the same way.

Other diners were nudging each other with their elbows and silently mouthing, "Look!" People's discomfort was more obvious than the aroma of curry floating from the kitchen.

Corbett and Marc both looked at me for reassurance that what they were seeing was actually happening. Marc leaned in close to me and asked, "Mom, is this one of those joke shows where they film you with hidden cameras?"

"I don't think so, honey," I answered.

I couldn't help but wonder if she ever had a job interview over lunch.

Corbett started to speak, but I interrupted him and changed the subject to avoid her overhearing something that I can only guess would have embarrassed us both.

She finished her salad with another three or four handfuls and was licking her fingers again when her carryout order was brought to the table. Motioning for the waitress to stay, she finished licking her fingertips, reached into her purse, and with the same hand that she had just licked clean, handed the now wide-eyed server a tip. She said "thank you," stood up, picked up her designer bag and her large to-go order, and walked out the door, the wind chimes clanking her departure.

You can be a captivating picture of grace and glamour, but if your social skills aren't in line with your image, people will judge you by your actions every time.

It's Hard Not to Notice

We enjoy eating and do it so often that sometimes we forget it's a bodily function. Other bodily functions having to do with our teeth or digestive system are attended to privately behind a bathroom door. Yet when we eat together, we're usually sitting less than two feet away from our tablemates. It's hard not to notice others' manners whether they're good or bad.

Chewing with our mouths open, burping, eating with our fingers when a fork is in order, slurping the milk in our cereal, blowing on our soup, chewing on ice cubes (okay, I'm guilty of that one, but I'm careful to make sure no one is around), and using our sleeve for a napkin might be doing what comes naturally. But we owe it to our children to help them replace these "natural" tendencies with the skills that will equip them to dine anywhere with ease and contemporary correctness.

We don't know where the Lord will lead them or whom He wants them to influence. If my sons end up on a foreign mission trip eating beans and rice out of a battered tin bowl with their fingers on the dirt floor of a shack, I want them to do so with grace. And if they find themselves in the senate dining room in Congress, I want them to dine next to the senator with their mind on their agenda, not on distractions: "Is my bread plate the one on my right or the one on my left?"

Learning good table manners and using them shows respect for and sensitivity to other people's comfort. Because we're sitting so close to each other, it's nice when everyone at the table is following the same table traditions.

Home is where we will have the most opportunities to use these manners and put thoughtfulness into action in a multitude of small ways. Home is our training ground. When we offer to refill our child's glass, we're considering her comfort. When she helps us with the dishes, she's doing the same for us. Each member of the family builds muscles of consideration and helpfulness.

What traditions of dining are relevant for today and provide for the comfort and convenience of everyone at the table? I'll mention several in this chapter and the next. When we put them into practice, our families will dine with ease and graciousness whether we're eating fast food on the go or dining at a five-star restaurant.

Being Served

In a formal restaurant, a server will set your plate down from your left and remove it from your right. (To help me remember this I keep in mind that both *right* and *remove* begin with the letter *R*.) The exception to this rule is beverages. All beverages are served and removed from your right. Your glass is to the right of your plate, so if drinks were served from the left, the waiter would have to reach across you with the pitcher to refill your beverage. Reducing the reach also reduces the chance of a pitcher of iced tea landing on your lap!

Why does it matter which way your food is served? It's nice knowing which way something is coming at you. The server is behind you when you're served, so knowing which way your food is going to be placed on the table allows you to move slightly out of the way in the other direction.

Passing Food

Salt and pepper. Even if your tablemate has only asked for the salt, pass the pepper too. Think of the salt and pepper as a married couple on their honeymoon who don't want to be apart for even a moment! (For children, call the salt and pepper best friends.) We pass them both in anticipation that the person might want the other in a moment. Also, we do it in preparation for the next person who asks for them. Saltshakers and pepper shakers are small, and it's easier to find and pass them along if they're kept together at the table. To keep hands from touching the tops of the shakers, shakers should not be handed to anyone. Instead, pick them up from the bottom and set them down on the table by the person next to you. He or she will do the same until they reach the person who asked for them.

Pass food to the right. During family meals where the food is set in bowls and platters, serve yourself from the bowl nearest you and pass it to your right. It's nice to hold the serving dish for people as they serve themselves. Food continues around the table until it reaches the person who originally served it. At some point during the meal, offer to pass the dish to anyone who would like some. "Would anyone like the broccoli casserole?"

Ask instead of reaching. If an item is farther away than your arm when it's extended, ask for it to be passed to you. When we reach for items, it's easy for our sleeves to get stains on them or for us to tip over our beverage or something else at the table.

Pass items with the handle facing the recipient. It's kind to pass items that have a handle such as a gravy boat, a mug or cup, and such by holding the item with the handle facing the recipient so he or she can easily grasp it.

Requesting Food

Try a little of everything. It's nice to put a little of everything on your plate unless you're allergic.

Don't hog your favorite. Avoid the temptation to pile your favorite food on your plate. Take a regular-size portion (one or two spoonfuls) first. After everyone has had an opportunity to have some you can help yourself again. (Children need special reminders about this when serving themselves snacks and desserts.)

Don't pile food on your plate. Teenage boys seem to need the most reminding about this. Take regular-size portions and then feel free to return after everyone has been served.

Ask for more without hesitation. Once everyone has been served, don't be shy about asking for seconds and thirds. You're actually paying the cook a compliment!

Dropping Silverware and Napkins

Dropped silverware. Everyone drops silverware now and then. At a restaurant, simply ask the server, "May I please have another fork?" There's no need to pick it up unless it fell where someone might trip over it. If you drop silverware at a friend's home, pick it up and ask the hostess, "I dropped my spoon. May I please have another?" If you drop the silverware at your own home—well, you know what to do. In my home, I say the ten-second rule was made for just such a situation!

Dropped napkin. If you drop your napkin and it hasn't been soiled by the floor, simply pick it up from the floor and place it on your lap, especially when dining in a home. In a restaurant, use your judgment. It's fine to ask for a replacement if you're uncomfortable with using it.

Surviving All Kinds of Spills

When you are the guest. If you spill a liquid in someone's home, bring it to the attention of the hostess and ask how you can help clean it up. Embarrassed, we might try to let it slide, but it's best to let her know quickly so a stain won't set in to her rug or table linens. In a restaurant, let a server know immediately if something spilled on the floor so that no one accidentally slips on it. If you drop food that won't stain while dining at a friend's home, leave it until after the meal, when you can pick it up at a less conspicuous time. At a restaurant you can leave the item on the floor if it's not in anyone's path.

When you are the hostess. As a hostess, take spills as a natural part of dining. If you're going to be upset if a particular tablecloth gets stained or a plate gets broken, don't use it. Also, keep in mind that your guest will probably feel embarrassed and sad about staining or breaking an item. Help put his mind at rest. "This was bought to be used. I expect it to be stained. Don't give it another thought. I'm not!" (But make sure you mean what you say!) If a guest offers to help you clean up a spill or stain, you may take him up on his offer if you need the extra help.

When something is spilled on a guest. Apologize immediately to the person and get paper towels, soda water, or whatever else is needed to help clean. Ask the person if you can be of assistance, but leave the cleaning to him.

Fixes for Breakages

When an item is damaged. As a guest, if you or a member of your family stains an item, offer to pay to have it professionally cleaned. If something gets broken, offer to replace it. As a hostess, thank your guest for her offer and turn her down. "That's not necessary, but you're very kind to offer." Regardless of the hostess saying it's not necessary, as a guest, you can always look for a similar item to replace it with. Give it to the hostess with a note saying how sorry you are, and explain that this item isn't quite the same but you hope she'll enjoy it. When my children return from a playdate or a meal with friends, I ask them if anything was broken. When their answer has been yes, I've called to apologize immediately and then replaced the item as soon as possible.

When a child carelessly breaks something. You can tell his parent about it if you feel led to do so. Perhaps she will be apologetic and offer to pay for damages. If she doesn't, there's not much you can do. Consider whether the cost is worth the risk of losing a friend for you and your child.

Wonder Words at the Table

"Please," "thank you," and "excuse me" are just as important and kind at the table as they are any other place. "Please" should be included in every request, and "thank you" should flow as freely as water.

One important thank-you is to the person who cooks our meal (or picks it up from the restaurant). To strengthen our gratefulness muscles, we should thank the person who provides every meal. "Thank you for bringing home Chick-fil-A, Dad," or "Thank you for the waffles, Mom." It's also nice to compliment the cook. "Dinner is delicious, Mrs. Bassoo, especially the curry!" If the food is less than tasty, you can still thank the hostess for preparing it for you. "Thank you for dinner, LauraBeth." If you're the guest for a meal out, compliment the hostess on choosing the restaurant. "Everything here is delicious, Mrs. Hull. You chose a great restaurant!"

"Thank you" communicates our understanding that the meal took time and energy to put together. To get up and walk away without comment is to dismiss the effort of those who worked on our behalf. "Dinner was delicious tonight, especially the lasagna. Thank you for everything, Shanna and Todd."

People of any age who leave the table temporarily should say "excuse me." If the reason is to go the bathroom, no explanation is needed. Children should ask to be excused before leaving the table. The reason? The adults might have a topic of discussion that's not been addressed yet. Asking first is also a sign of kindness and respect, which is why adults should do the same.

When dining at home, each person should clear her own place setting, putting the dishes in the sink or dishwasher. After that, your house rules for who helps clean should be followed without arguing. Others should offer to help simply because assisting is nice and it encourages others to do the same. "I know it's your night to clean up, Brooke. I'll help you!"

How Long Should Dinner Last?

When dining, we should be aware of children's short attention span. For a three-year-old, ten to fifteen minutes is a successful dinnertime. Keeping mealtimes short for our littlest ones helps them enjoy successful meals with good manners intact. Dinnertime is so important that from the youngest age we want our children to look forward to it—a place of encouragement, peace, laughter, and family bonding.

Mom to Mom

Each year I buy an inexpensive plain color vinyl tablecloth for use once a month and for all holidays in the year. In the center of the tablecloth I write the year and our family motto: Mc-Kees—Together Forever! Each family member has a permanent marker (in a signature color!) and writes on the tablecloth something that has happened during the month. It's a fun and unique journal of our family life. It's been heartwarming watching the boys' handwriting change from pre-K scribbles to cursive. I cherish their drawings—from their toddler doodles to their pictures of knights, superheroes, and sports cars. The things recorded would, I'm certain, be forgotten if we would not have written them. Marc getting an *A* on his first algebra quiz, Corbett learning to swim, Daddy getting a new client, me writing my first blog post, our trip to the river to watch the manatees, and lots of answers to prayers. All are reminders of the joys of everyday life and our wellspring of reasons to be grateful.

To experience these benefits, children need to make mealtime a no-fussing zone, and we need to make it be a no-nagging zone. We're all most likely to succeed when mealtimes are short. Increase the length of your child's time at the table by about five minutes per year until he or she is seven or older. By seven, barring any issues such as ADD or the like, children should be able to sit for a family meal of 30 minutes.

Respecting Those Who Serve

Teach your children the importance of showing kindness and respect to those who serve them. Without servers, we'd never have the special treat of eating out. Give them the gift of your full attention when they're at your table. Smile, make eye contact, and thank them for seeing to your comfort and care by taking your order, bringing your food, refilling your drinks, clearing your plates, and anything else they do.

When a server shares the specials of the day, teach your child not to make a negative face. Hearing that braised brussels sprouts are the vegetable of the day might make your child want to twist his face with a double "yuck," but responding to people with silly faces and negative comments hurts their feelings.

I still have to remind my boys in advance (although I need to do it less and less these days), "Show your hearts to the server." From previous conversations they know that servers' hard work for us is often overlooked. We want our family to be the cool breeze in someone's day, so I remind the boys before a server comes to the table, "Remember to let the server know your heart." It's fun to see the server respond positively to our kindness. So many times, we've had a waiter or waitress say, "Thank you for being so nice. You've made my night."

Because we say grace before meals, including in restaurants, we want to make sure we represent Christ well as His ambassadors when dining out. We make sure to tip generously—at least 20 percent. We do it because God gives so freely to us that it would be a poor representation of Him to give stingily.

If a server isn't giving stellar service, I don't take it personally. Instead, I remind myself that I'm an ambassador for Christ, and I try hard to turn his day around by going the extra mile to bring the smile and considerate words of Christ into the room. If there is a problem, ask to speak to the manager. The manager has a relationship with the associate, so his words will ring truer with the server. If you share your concern directly to the waiter, he simply ends up with a bad opinion of you, and no positive change in attitude or service will result.

It's Hard Not to Notice

When sitting just a foot or two away from others at the table, it's hard not to notice their manners—whether they are good or bad. Paying attention to the way we handle ourselves at the table is a gift to our tablemates and shows our respect for others and ourselves. When we use good manners, we're purposefully regarding others' sensitivities and caring about their comfort.

Life is shocking enough. Our meals can be havens from the noise and stress of the outside world. When we're all using the same traditions and attending to each other's well-being, mealtimes nurture our communion with one another. They are opportunities for us to express our gratitude for God, who so lovingly provides the food, and for the people who graciously prepare and serve it. As a result, joy overflows in blessing and conversation.

Inspiration and Application

1. "Listen carefully to what I am saying—and be wary of the shrewd advice that tells you how to get ahead in the world on your own. Giving, not getting, is the way. Generosity begets generosity. Stinginess impoverishes" (Mark 4:24-25). We should be generous in helping those in need with our financial resources. There are many other ways we can give. Using manners is a way of giving generously of ourselves. Do you agree with this statement? Why or why not?

2. "Generosity begets generosity. Stinginess impoverishes." What happens to the personality and character of a person who gives of himself generously and one who gives stingily?

3. We are learning lots of wonderful table traditions and manners. It's time to plan a fun dining tutorial for your family. Pick a night and record the date and time here. Also, list your menu of family favorites you'll prepare and the special treat you'll provide for your children in celebration of their new dining knowledge. (It's fun to have a dollar-store item wrapped and laid at each place setting, to be opened after dinner, as a memory-making reminder of your special family dinnertime.) Plan your dinner in the space below.

   Day: Date: Time:

   First course:

   Main course:

   Dessert:

   Beverage:

   Roll or bread:

   Wrapped gift:

   Skills I'll introduce during dinner:

4. Review the instructions in this chapter about how to pass food around the table. Make notes to jog your memory and then begin putting this into practice at your first tutorial meal.

5. Dining accidents are as predictable as death and taxes. Review how to graciously handle some of the most common ones we talked about in this chapter and share them with your children at a meal sometime within the next few days.

17

Dining Do's, Don'ts, and How-To's

A man's manners are a mirror in which he shows his portrait.
JOHANN WOLFGANG VON GOETHE

Etiquette IQ Quiz

1. The foil surrounding a baked potato...

   A. should be removed in the kitchen prior to the potato being placed on your plate

   B. should be removed by the diner prior to eating his potato

   C. should be left on the potato to help keep it warm while it is being eaten

2. To eat a dinner roll...

   A. Tear it in half, butter a half at a time, and take a bite from the buttered half.

   B. Slice it in half horizontally, butter each half, and take a bite from the buttered half.

   C. Tear off and butter one bite at a time.

3. Soup is spooned...

   A. toward you only when eaten from a cup

   B. toward you only when eaten from a soup bowl or plate

   C. away from you when eaten from a cup, soup bowl, or plate*

Answers: 1) A 2) C 3) C.*

It's no fun when food gets the best of us! And boy, at least for me, it can do that in a hundred different ways.

When I was barely five years old, my mom took me to an Italian restaurant. I was wearing a white sundress with embroidered daises. We had picked it out together at Montgomery Ward. When I twirled in it, I felt like a princess. It was the first piece of clothing I remember wearing.

During dinner, an errant meatball rolled off my plate, onto my lap, and onto the floor. It came to a slow halt by the table next to us. I did what any five-year-old would do in that case: I got up, picked up the meatball, and took a bite out of it. The people at the next table chuckled. My mom thinks it's cute now. At that moment, not so much.

She thought I began crying from her scolding, and part of me was. The other part of me was crying because I noticed the red trail of sauce that had marked the meatball's path to freedom right through the middle of the biggest and prettiest daisy on my dress.

Sadly, my stories of food mishaps don't end there. I've had my share as an adult too. A roll once flew out of my hand and knocked over someone's water glass. Another time, the majority of the food on my plate slid onto the heirloom tablecloth of a pastor's wife as she was introducing me to speak before an audience of 250 attentive guests.

How to Eat Some of Our Favorite Foods

I suppose we all have our stories of mishaps and questions about how to eat certain foods. I get lots of questions about eating spaghetti (my response is the most commonly read article on my blog), baked potatoes, soup, cupcakes, and other favorites. Here's how we can eat them with the biggest chance of the food making it into our mouths without any detours to our clothes, the tablecloth, or our neighbor's table!

Bacon. As long as the bacon is crisp, it's a finger food. No knife and fork needed.

Baked potatoes. The foil should be removed prior to the potato being placed on your plate. If it's not, remove it completely, fold it in fourths, and set it on the side of your plate or on your bread plate. Place butter first on your bread plate and then on your potato, not directly from the butter serving dish to your potato. Use your fork to transfer the butter to your potato. Add salt and pepper and any other toppings. Gently mix these with your fork to distribute them throughout the potato. Eat the white flesh with your fork. If you'd like to eat the potato skin as well, that's fine. Use your knife and fork to cut the potato with skin, one bite at a time.

Bananas. If served sliced, eat it with your fork. If eaten whole, peel the banana about one-third of the way. When that is eaten, peel another one-third, eating each as you go.

Biscuits, bread, and rolls. For rolls, tear off and butter one bite at a time. When you finish one bite and are ready for the next, tear and then butter it. Don't cut or tear the roll in half. For soft breadsticks, tear off one bite at a time; don't put the breadstick in your mouth like a cigar. Slices of bread are buttered and eaten without tearing off a bite-size piece first. For biscuits, cut the biscuit in half and butter each half while it's warm. Eat it as you would a slice of bread.

Cake. Lay the slice of cake on its side and eat it with your fork. If it's served with ice cream, use your spoon to push the ice cream onto your fork.

Candy. When picking up candy (or any food item) served in a paper frill, take the frill as well as the candy.

Cereal. Eat cereal with milk with a large spoon. Do not drink any leftover milk directly from the bowl. Use your spoon. Cereal can be crunchy, so it's often a noisy food to eat. Be extra cautious of making noises. Take small bites, chew with your mouth tightly closed, and don't slurp the milk.

Chicken. Fried chicken is a finger food regardless of where it's served. It's considered a casual food, so you won't normally find it served at formal events. If you're in a restaurant where silverware is at your place setting, and your prefer to eat it with your knife and fork, you may. Baked chicken is eaten with a knife and fork. For children, chicken nuggets are always finger foods. Adults should use a knife and fork with a fancier variation of a nugget if the utensils are provided.

Condiments and dips. Place dips on your plate first. Don't dip your food directly into the dip bowl. Pour sauces and gravies over the food you're eating or on the side of your plate to dip each bite into with your fork. At fast-food restaurants, take only the number of condiments you think you'll use and never allow your child to play with them or open them in such a manner that the condiment packet might explode.

Corn on the cob. Like fried chicken, this is a causal finger food. To avoid butter running off the cob and down your arm, put butter and salt and pepper on just one section of rows of the cob at a time. Eat that section from left to right and then butter and salt and pepper the next area. Place the butter on the side of your dinner plate.

Cupcakes and muffins. If you're sitting down with a plate, remove the cupcake or muffin completely from the wrapper. Fold large wrappers in fourths and set them on the side of your plate or on your bread plate. Cut regular-size cupcakes or muffins into fourths. Use your fingers to eat. If the frosting on the cupcake is messy, you may use your fork. Mini muffins and cupcakes can be eaten with the fingers in a bite or two.

Danish and other pastries. These may be eaten with your fingers or with a knife and fork if you prefer.

Deviled eggs. At picnics and other informal affairs, these are finger foods. You may use a knife and fork if you prefer when they're served for Sunday dinner, Easter, or other more formal occasions. (Some of us call these "stuffed eggs" just so we don't give the devil any credit!)

French fries. These are the ultimate finger food. Eat them one at a time unless they are shoestring fries. Dip fries into ketchup; don't pour ketchup over the fries. Steak fries are eaten with a knife and fork unless served in a fast-food restaurant, food cart or truck, or other casual setting.

Pizza. Unless it's deep-dish, pizza is a finger food. You may use a knife and fork if you prefer, especially while the pizza is extra hot. It's fine to fold large slices in half to eat with your fingers. Deep-dish pizza is always eaten with a knife and fork.

Ravioli. Use a knife and fork.

Salad. Use a knife and fork to cut the salad one bite at a time. Cut any leaves that won't fit easily into your mouth. If cherry tomatoes are served in the salad that are too big to be eaten in one bite, pierce the skin of the tomato gently to allow the juices to escape without exploding out. Once the skin is pierced, cut the tomato in half to eat.

Sandwiches. Open-faced sandwiches are eaten with a knife and fork. If a sandwich is too large to bite into comfortably, remove the top piece of bread and place it on the side of your plate. Eat the now open-face sandwich with your knife and fork. If you want, you can then eat the top piece of bread with your fingers. For burgers and hot dogs served in paper wrappers in casual restaurants, you may remove the wrapper completely or, if you feel the sandwich might drip, fold down the wrapper by about one-third and eat from the wrapper, unfolding as you go.

Shrimp. When served as shrimp cocktail with the tails on, it is a finger food. Eat the shrimp in one or two bites, and lay the shell on the plate underneath the shrimp cocktail dish. Do not place the tails back into the cocktail glass. If the shrimp are too large to eat in a bite or two, place the shrimp on the under plate and use your knife and fork to cut and eat one bite at a time. If a seafood fork is given, use it to hold the shrimp as you eat them instead of holding them in your fingers. Fried shrimp are also finger foods. The same manners apply when eating them as when enjoying shrimp cocktail. If the shrimp are served as part of a pasta dish or any other way such as shrimp scampi, they are cut with a knife and eaten with a fork.

Shish kebabs and other foods on a stick. When food is served skewered on a stick, remove the food all at once, using your fork to push it off the skewer. Lay the empty skewer on the side of your plate. Then use your knife and fork to cut and eat one bite at a time.

Soup. Soup can be served in cups, bowls, or soup plates. If served with an under plate, the spoon rests on the under plate between bites and when finished. Do not blow on soup (or any other food or beverage). Instead, wait for it to cool. If adding crackers, add just enough for one or two bites. Don't make a mush of the soup by crumbling a handful of saltines or floating lots of oyster or fish crackers. Sip soup from the side of your soupspoon so it won't all come splashing down on you. (Stews, chili, and other chunky-type soups and such are eaten from the front of the spoon.) Spoon the soup away from you in the bowl. This might seem counterintuitive, but if any soup spills from your spoon, it is more likely to land in the bowl instead of your lap.

Mom to Mom

One of Kent's friends had a humdinger of a party for his thirty-fifth birthday. About 150 guests gathered at the country club his wife had booked for the evening meal of heavy appetizers and lots of dancing to work them off. There weren't any chairs, so people ate standing up. The waitstaff should have set out lots of trays to dispose of the many toothpicks and small paper napkins that replaced the plates that evening. However, they didn't. I watched people place the toothpicks in potted plants, hide them behind and under sofa cushions, stick them in their pockets and purses, and place them on servers' trays as they passed by— trays newly refilled with food.

What should you and I do in this case? There are a couple of good options. We can stop a server as he or she walks by and ask, "I don't see a place to put my used napkin and toothpicks. Where should I place them?" That's a nice way to let the staff know they need to set out some wastebaskets or trays for discards. The second option, if you don't see a server, is to dispose of the items in the bathroom wastebasket. There's no need to carry them home in your purse or pocket!

Spaghetti. When cooking spaghetti at home, I break the noodles in half or thirds prior to boiling them to make them easier for my children to manage. Regardless of the length of the noodles, when they're ready to eat, using your fork, separate a few strands at a time and twirl them around your fork, bringing the fork to your mouth without any dangling pasta. If you're given a spoon with the spaghetti you may use it. If you're not given one, don't ask for one. In parts of Italy, eating spaghetti with a spoon is considered bad manners. Some restaurants honoring that Italian tradition follow suit.

Starches and vegetables. Once a child has the manual dexterity to use a fork comfortably, all starches and vegetables are eaten with a fork. This includes peas, corn off the cob, rice, mashed potatoes, and such. A bite of roll or bread may be used to help push the food onto the fork. Use bread only, not your knife or fingers!

The Best of the Do's and Don'ts

I have listed here the most other-centered do's and don'ts of dining. Let's start with the don'ts and end on a high note with the do's.

Dining Don'ts

Don't blow on food. Allow it to cool on its own. We need to keep our breath to ourselves.

Don't cut more than one or two bites of your food at a time. It's fine to cut the food all at once for your children.

Don't mix the food on your plate. You're eating off a plate, not from a blender.

Don't pile your plate too full. Make multiple trips to the buffet table or serve yourself seconds instead.

Don't place anything not related to eating on the table. Keep electronics, papers, and purses off the table.

Don't place your elbows on the table. You may place them on the table when no food is present. However, you maintain better table posture if you keep your elbows off the table. Only allow your elbows on the table in causal situations.

Don't overfill your fork or spoon. What goes on the fork or spoon needs to go into your mouth in one bite. Don't bring the utensil out of your mouth with food still on it.

Don't chew with your mouth open. Also, don't chew ice at the table. Take extra-small bites of all crunchy foods. This saves your tablemates from having to hear your chewing noises.

Don't gesture with silverware. When you're not eating, place your knife and fork in the resting position.

Don't groom yourself at the table. Don't apply lipstick, use a toothpick, or fiddle with your hair at the table. Grooming is done in the bathroom. Gentlemen, even young ones, don't flip their ties over their shoulders while eating.

Don't push your plate away from you when you're done eating. Signal that you're finished eating by placing your knife and fork side by side using the finished signal (ten o'clock).

Don't feed pets at the table. (In full disclosure, on this one, you'll need to do as I say, not do as I do. Sorry, but my dog has the most beautiful brown eyes. How can I say no? At the kitchen table, she knows she has a friend in me. But in the dining room, she knows there is no use in batting her doggie eyes at me.)

Don't talk about diets, restaurants, or other foods while eating. The host will feel as if she served the wrong menu or picked the wrong restaurant for you.

Don't dunk in public. Do your dunking when you're at home.

Dining Do's

Thank the person who prepared your meal. Also, if it's sincere, compliment the cook on a job well done.

When trying food samples in a store, step away from the table to eat. Remember to thank the server. There will be a trash bin near the serving table where you can throw your napkin or toothpick away. Make sure to dispose of the item there instead of leaving it in the cart or anywhere else.

Place a serving utensil on the plate beside each buffet dish. At a restaurant, serving utensils do not go back into the large serving dish. Instead, place the utensil on the small plate that should be by each dish.

Remove loud children. If a child cannot sit still or is being loud, remove him from the table. Another's right to expect a fuss- and cry-free meal trumps our right to disturb everyone nearby. If a child (or adult) can clearly be heard at other tables, he is being disruptive. The finer the restaurant, the more quickly the child should be removed.

Try a bite of everything. Unless you're allergic, try all the food the hostess has spent time and effort making for your enjoyment.

Take small bites. This way you can join in the conversation at any moment.

Wait until you have swallowed what you're eating before taking a drink. Also, wipe your lips with your napkin before taking a drink to keep food stains from the outside of the glass or cup.

Remove bones, gristle, seeds, pits, and such carefully. If the item went into your mouth with your fork or spoon, try to gently push the item back onto your fork or spoon to remove it from your mouth. If this is difficult (it often is) use your thumb and first finger. In either case, place the item on the side of your plate. It's nice to hide them next to the parsley or other garnish if possible.

Bring the food up to your lips. Don't bend over in order to eat.

Ask for items to be passed to you. Reaching is liable to cause spills.

Get a new plate each time you return to the buffet table. This is always true when dining in a restaurant. However, when eating in someone's home, note how many plates there are. Usually you will use the same plate for everything except dessert.

Know what you want before stepping in line to order. When dining at a fast-food restaurant, know what everyone in your group wants to order before stepping into line. This avoids those behind you from having to wait.

Respect the drive-through staff. Take off your sunglasses when speaking with them, don't ignore them by talking on your cell phone, and have your payment handy so the line moves swiftly. Also, go inside for large orders in consideration of the drivers in line behind you.

Enjoying Every Meal

Our shared dining traditions rest on the foundation of caring for others and seeing to their comfort. They unite us in a very special way and develop important traits in our children: consideration, respect, self-control, patience, attention to detail, and sharing of their time and attention with others.

In this chapter and the preceding three, we mentioned a lot of dining manners. The good news is that if you maintain consistent expectations, reinforce your children's good behavior with encouragement, incorporate new manners at appropriate ages and stages, and most importantly, model them yourself at every meal, your children will grow into teens and adults who will enjoy every meal. They'll be confident and at ease whether they are eating fast food on the go or dining at the finest restaurant in town. If they are enjoying their first date, attending a job interview, or proposing or being proposed to, they'll be able to be present emotionally and enjoy the moment and the thing that matters most at the table—the people with them.

Inspiration and Application

1. "This most generous God who gives seed to the farmer that becomes bread for your meals is more than extravagant with you. He gives you something you can then give away, which grows into full-formed lives, robust in God, wealthy in every way, so that you can be generous in every way, producing with us great praise to God" (2 Corinthians 9:10-11). Here we read about God's extravagance in giving to us. How can you respond to the generosity God has shown you?

2. You have probably been blessed in so many ways. You have children, a soft and safe place to sleep, and food for yourself and your family. Oh, how many people in the world would gladly change places with you or me right this minute! How does this knowledge of the wealth you have impact the way you feel about giving of yourself?

3. We can give so much of ourselves that we empty our own pantry. What are two ways we can learn to restock our spiritual cupboards so they're never bare? From what you know of Scripture and from reading the verse above again, list two ways.

4. As you read "How to Eat Some of Our Favorite Foods," which three items do you want to begin showing your children how to eat differently?

5. Which three "Dining Don'ts" are you going to begin implementing with your family?

6. Which three "Dining Do's" are you going to start with?

Encouragement
and Blessings

I will hold myself to a standard
of grace, not perfection.
UNKNOWN

How is it that we've come so quickly to this point? You are very kind to have read to the end of the book! Thank you for sticking with me. I hope you've enjoyed our time together. I feel honored to be able to share with you what I've learned about imparting kindhearted manners to our children.

Did you notice that we have a lot in common? We love our children. We want to bring out the best in them so they can enjoy a lifetime of happy and healthy relationships. We want them to have great friends and to be great friends. We want them to be likable and well-liked. And we want what was said of the Lord in Luke 2:52 (NIV) to be said of our children: "Jesus grew in wisdom and stature, and in favor with God and man."

Our children will live in our homes only about 21 percent of our lives. That's our window of opportunity to impart everything we want them to know so they can soar through life on their own. My prayer for you as I've written this book has been that it would be your guide for equipping your children to live out the apostle Paul's description of love: patience and kindness.

Life isn't made up of grand gestures and extravagant events. It's marked by humble days full of little moments in which smiles, kindnesses, and small obligations done by glad habit win the hearts of others and preserve our own. And that is what etiquette is all about—paying attention to the small moments because you understand they are the ones that matter, especially to moms like you and me.

May the Lord bless your home every day with laughter and love and sweet moments. May it be filled with grace and graciousness. If I can be of assistance, I'm easy to find online. I hope we get the chance to meet in person one day. Until then...

Blessings,

Maralee Mckee

Maralee's Best
Zucchini Bread

Great manners and great recipes have something in common. They both allow you to know you're sharing your best. After my first taste of zucchini bread I knew I wanted to find a recipe for it that produced the same moist, delicious, hearty bread so I could bake loaves for my friends and family anytime. In my search, I tried multiple recipes. All of them were okay, but none of them made me say, "This is worth every calorie!"—until I tasted this recipe. Once I tried it, my search was over.

I have a collection of recipes like this in my recipe box. I call them "Recipes that Wow!" They've passed the taste test, and I'm certain my guests will find them delicious. Knowing I have a treasure box of best recipes at my ready helps me feel confident and at ease serving guests.

So it is with the "recipes" of good manners. Whether it's the Five-Star First Impression, the four elements of a gracious thank-you note, the rest and finished signals of dining, or any of the other multitude of manners in this book, knowing I have these treasured skills at my ready is comforting. Good manners can be thought of as the tried-and-true "recipes" for sharing the best of yourself with others.

Maralee's Best Zucchini Bread

Preheat oven to 350 degrees. Liberally spray three small loaf pans (approximately 6 by 3½ inches) with nonstick cooking spray.

Ingredients

3 eggs

2 cups sugar

1 cup vegetable oil

2½ cups peeled and shredded zucchini (approximately six small to medium zucchini)

2 teaspoons vanilla

1 teaspoon salt

1 teaspoon baking soda

1 teaspoon baking powder

1 teaspoon cinnamon

3 cups all-purpose flour

1 cup shredded coconut

1 cup toasted and chopped pecans (break pecans into bite-sized pieces with your hands)

Stir ingredients in the order given in a large mixing bowl. Stir lightly with a large spoon after adding each ingredient.

Bake for 30 to 35 minutes or until a toothpick inserted into the middle of the loaf comes out clean. Do not allow pans to touch in the oven.

Cool on a wire rack for 15 minutes and then invert onto a serving dish. When completely cool, wrap loaves in plastic wrap to keep moist and fresh.

Manners That Matter
for Moms
Top-100 Checklist

We want our children to grow in their ability to be at ease, confident, and thoughtful in their interactions. Here are some of the most important manners we have covered in this book that you'll want to prayerfully pass along to your children as you seek to give them the skills they need to thrive on their own as adults who are rooted in Christ, secure in who they are, and well-liked and respected by their peers. Check off the manners your children use regularly. Check off remaining boxes as your children master each skill. Keep in mind that some of the manners won't be mastered until the high school years.

First Impressions and Greetings
- [ ] stands to greet
- [ ] smiles
- [ ] sees (makes eye contact)
- [ ] shakes hands
- [ ] speaks welcoming words

Introducing Yourself and Others
- [ ] knows the three steps of introducing yourself
- [ ] knows the four steps of introducing others
- [ ] uses people's names in introductions and conversation
- [ ] responds kindly when being introduced
- [ ] knows whose name to say first in an introduction
- [ ] can introduce himself or others to a group
- [ ] uses titles and honorifics
- [ ] knows what to say when forgetting someone's name

Conversational Skills

- ☐ THINKs before speaking
- ☐ understands the body language basics
- ☐ actively listens
- ☐ doesn't regularly brag, gossip, tease, or whisper
- ☐ knows how to start a conversation
- ☐ asks questions that invite others to talk about themselves
- ☐ answers questions in complete sentences
- ☐ answers and asks questions to keep conversations going

Compliments

- ☐ understands that compliments are gifts
- ☐ gives sincere compliments
- ☐ receives compliments graciously
- ☐ understands the difference between compliments and flattery
- ☐ knows when to give compliments

Wonder Words

- ☐ regularly uses the six most common Wonder Words
- ☐ understands the meaning of *thank you*
- ☐ understands the meaning of *please*
- ☐ knows that using Wonder Words is something we never outgrow

Gracious Guests and Great Hosts

- ☐ knows the basic elements included on an invitation
- ☐ invites only a reasonable number of people to a party
- ☐ greets guests at the door
- ☐ divides time between guests
- ☐ offers refreshments
- ☐ makes guests feel included
- ☐ allows guests to go first
- ☐ helps cleans up after a guest leaves and before leaving a host's home
- ☐ plans ahead when hosting guests
- ☐ doesn't wander through a host's home
- ☐ speaks to others in a host's home
- ☐ participates in the party activities

Gives and Receives Gifts Gleefully

☐ opens cards before opening gifts
☐ comments nicely and says "thank you" after opening a gift
☐ pays attention to each gift
☐ considers the recipient's tastes when choosing a gift

Growing in Gratitude

☐ knows the four-step formula for writing thank-you notes
☐ knows when to send thank-you notes
☐ expresses gratitude for gifts through the best medium
☐ expresses gratitude freely and frequently

Bathroom and Bodily Noise Etiquette

☐ always flushes
☐ knows when to use a friendly flush
☐ knows what to say after burping
☐ knows what to say if someone else burps
☐ knows what to say after passing gas
☐ knows what to say if someone else passes gas
☐ knows how to cover a sneeze or cough
☐ knows what to say after someone sneezes
☐ knows when to leave the table due to a cold

Dining Skills for Growing Strong Families

☐ understands the importance of dining together
☐ knows the three items to the right of the plate in a family place setting
☐ knows the three items to the left of the plate in a family place setting
☐ knows where to add the salad fork to the left of the place setting
☐ knows what will be added for a fairly formal place setting
☐ recognizes a dessertspoon and dessert fork above the plate
☐ can set a family place setting
☐ can set a fairly formal place setting

FUNdamentals of Dining and Secret Signals

☐ knows the rest signal with a fork
☐ knows the rest signal with a knife

☐ knows the rest signal with a napkin
☐ knows the finished signal with a fork
☐ knows the finished signal with a knife
☐ knows the finished signal with a napkin
☐ knows in which direction to enter and exit a chair
☐ knows how to give or receive assistance with a chair when
   being seated
☐ uses the table checker
☐ has good posture at the table
☐ knows how to place a napkin on the lap
☐ uses the napkin throughout the meal
☐ understands how to hold the knife and fork
☐ knows how to cut food properly
☐ knows the zigzag style of dining

Fast Food to Five-Star Dining

☐ passes food to others
☐ knows how to serve at the table
☐ handles spills and breakage at the table without panic
☐ maintains appropriate conversation at the table
☐ knows the etiquette of saying grace

Dining Do's, Don'ts, and How-To's

☐ eats a baked potato properly
☐ knows the etiquette of eating biscuits, bread, and rolls
☐ knows how to butter, season, and eat corn on the cob
☐ knows when french fries are and are not finger food
☐ knows how to eat large sandwiches and burgers
☐ knows how to properly spoon and sip soup
☐ doesn't blow on food to cool it off
☐ doesn't overfill the plate, fork, or spoon
☐ knows not to groom at the table
☐ does not use electronics at the table
☐ knows how to remove seeds, gristle, bones, and such from the mouth
☐ knows the etiquette of dining in restaurants and others' homes
☐ raises food to the lips instead of bending down to it

Notes

Chapter 3: A Gentle Word and a Tender Way

1. See Sarah Chana Radcliffe, "The Positive/Negative Ratio," *Aish.com*. www.aish.com/f/p/48918197.html.

Chapter 4: The Five-Star First Impression

1. Michael Solomon, cited in Sue Barrett, "First Impressions," *Evancharmichael.com*. www.evancarmichael.com/Sales/4476/First-Impressions.html.

Chapter 5: How Do You Do Your "How-Do-You-Do's?"

1. "Developmental Milestones: Understanding words, behavior, and concepts," *Babycenter*. www.babycenter.com/0_developmental-milestones-understanding-words-behavior-and-co_6575.bc.

Chapter 7: Conversation Skills—What You Say and How You Say It

1. Debi LaPlante and Nalini Ambady, "Saying It Like It Isn't: Mixed Messages from Men and Women in the Workplace," *Journal of Applied Social Psychology 32* (2002), 2435-57. Cited in Hamilton Gregory, *Public Speaking for College and Career* (New York: McGraw-Hill, 2010), 284.

2. Gretchen Rubin, *The Happiness Project: Or, Why I Spent a Year Trying to Sing in the Morning, Clean My Closets, Fight Right, Read Aristotle, and Generally Have More Fun* (New York: HarperCollins, 2009), 156.

Chapter 9: Wonder Words and the Wonders They Work

1. Life Application Study Bible NIV (Wheaton: Tyndale House, 1997). See note on Proverbs 26:9.

Chapter 12: Growing in Gratitude

1. Interview with Christine Carter, "Change Your Kid's Attitude with Gratitude," *Greater Good: the Science of a Meaningful Life*. www.greatergood.berkeley.edu/gg _live/parenting_videos/video/change_your_kids_attitude_with_gratitude/.com.

Chapter 13: Bathroom and Bodily Noise Etiquette...Oh My!

1. Wiki.answers.com/Q/How_much_gas_does_the_human_body_release_over _the_course_of_its_life_time.

Chapter 14: Life Skills Learned at the Dining Table

1. This study and the two that follow are cited in Jill Kimball, *Drawing Families Together, One Meal at a Time* (Orlando, FL: Active Media Publishing, LLC, 2003), 16-17.

Bibliography

Borba, Michele. *The Big Book of Parenting Solutions: 101 Answers to Your Everyday Challenges and Wildest Worries.* San Francisco: Jossey-Bass, 2009.

———. *Building Moral Intelligence: The Seven Essential Virtues That Teach Kids to Do the Right Thing.* San Francisco: Jossey-Bass, 2001.

Forni, P.M. *Choosing Civility: The Twenty-Five Rules of Considerate Conduct.* New York: St. Martin's Press, 2002.

Kimball, Jill. *Drawing Families Together, One Meal at a Time.* Orlando: Active Media, 2003.

Moore, June Hines. *You Can Raise a Well-Mannered Child.* Nashville: Broadman & Holman, 1996.

Rubin, Gretchen. *The Happiness Project: Or, Why I Spent a Year Trying to Sing in the Morning, Clean My Closets, Fight Right, Read Aristotle, and Generally Have More Fun.* New York: HarperCollins, 2009.

Samalin, Nancy. *Loving Without Spoiling: And 100 Other Timeless Tips for Raising Terrific Kids.* New York: MJF Books, 2003.

Wallace, Carol McD. *Elbows Off the Table, Napkin in the Lap, No Video Games During Dinner: The Modern Guide to Teaching Children Good Manners.* New York: St. Martin's Press, 1996.

Acknowledgments

What better way to end a book about living out graciousness and gratitude than by saying "thank you"! I wrote the words in this book with the encouragement, help, and wisdom of special people in my life. It's a joy to express my gratefulness to each of them.

To Debbie Poulalion: You are my anchor and lighthouse for every word I write. Thank you for partnering with me these past six years. I admire and cherish your perseverance, insight, ideas, and attention to detail. You are a delight, and our friendship is a blessing I hold dear.

To Janie Upchurch: Your Christlike example inspires me. Thank you for your prayers on my behalf and for the daily notes of encouragement. Your kindness strengthened and sustained me.

To Tia Friedman: Some people say when you write a book, you should picture yourself at a table with coffee, talking to your best friend. You were the person in the movie theater of my mind. We weren't able to enjoy our Starbuck's Frappuccinos together, but I wrote this book drinking a lot of imaginary ones with you. You mean the world to me.

To Angela Hull: I admire, appreciate, and cherish you. Thank you for bringing the Manners Mentor brand to life. Your artistry is spectacular. Your friendship and love are even more so.

To Chip MacGregor: You were so kind to speak to this newbie writer, catch my vision, and work to put this book into the hands of the people who would bring it to life. I'm grateful and honored to be working with you.

To the Harvest House Team: Thank you for embracing my Manners Matter message. I'm thankful and humbled to be part of the Harvest House family. A special thank you to Gene Skinner. You are so kind to share your time, talent, and expertise with me.

To Christy Jordan: You are an inspiration! Thank you for showing me how to make sweet tea and a hundred of the best foods I've ever tasted. Your loving work has helped me fill my family's tummies with delicious food and their hearts with future fond memories of Mom's cooking. Thank you for writing the foreword to this book. It's the sweetest gift of friendship you could have given me.

To the Manners Mentor Facebook family: Our time together each day is something I cherish. Thank you for joining me in spreading the word that manners matter. You understand that we make our part of the world better when we show God's love through our words and actions. May you each be blessed tenfold. You are dear.

To my many students and clients: I'm grateful to each of you. It's an honor to be your Manners Mentor.

To my family near and far: I hope you know how much I love and cherish each of you. I'm glad we do life together!

And lastly, to my mom: I love you! Thank you for being there, for listening, for leading, and for loving. You are a blessing! I love you "45," and I'm so glad you know that means my love is immeasurable!

About the Author

Maralee McKee is the Manners Mentor. Her heart's desire is to inspire, encourage, and train people to turn their self-consciousness into self-confidence and to interact with kindness, grace, and other-centeredness as ambassadors for Christ in a fast-paced, casual, techno-savvy culture. Maralee is a popular speaker at women's organizations, church groups, and corporate events. She is a frequent guest on TV and radio and has been featured in numerous newspapers and magazines. She is the creator of the Manners Mentor curriculum for children and teens ages five through fourteen. Her greatest blessing is being Kent's wife and mother to Marc and Corbett.

Find more information about Maralee:
www.MannersMentor.com
Facebook: Manners.Mentor
Twitter: MannersMentor
Pinterest: Maralee_McKee